THE YELLOW BOOK

COLORWORKS 3

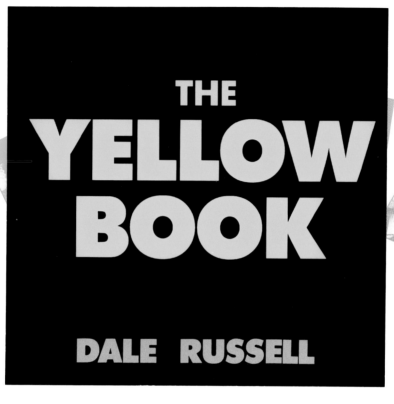

THE
YELLOW
BOOK

DALE RUSSELL

NORTH
LIGHT
BOOKS

Cincinnati, Ohio

A QUARTO BOOK

Copyright © 1990 Quarto Publishing plc
First published in the U.S.A. by North Light Books, an imprint
of F & W Publications, Inc.
1507 Dana Avenue
Cincinnati, Ohio 45207

ISBN 0-89134-335-0

This book was designed and produced by
Quarto Publishing plc
The Old Brewery
6 Blundell Street
London N7 9BH

SENIOR EDITOR Sally MacEachern
EDITORS Paula Borthwick, Eleanor van Zandt
DESIGNERS Penny Dawes, David Kemp, Julia King, Karin Skånberg
PICTURE MANAGER Joanna Wiese
PICTURE RESEARCH ADMINISTRATION Prue Reilly
PHOTOGRAPHERS Martin Norris, Phil Starling

ART DIRECTOR Moira Clinch
EDITORIAL DIRECTOR Carolyn King

Manufactured in Hong Kong by Regent Publishing Services Ltd
Typeset by Ampersand Typesetting Ltd, Bournemouth
Printed in Hong Kong by C & C Joint Printing Co. (H.K.) Ltd

DEDICATION
With great love, I would like to thank my husband Steve for
patiently guiding me through the days and nights overtaken by
color and my daughter Lucy Scarlett for remaining happy
while color came first.

The color tints printed in this book have been checked and
are, to the publisher's knowledge, correct. The publisher can
take no responsibility for errors that might have occurred.

CONTENTS

Using Colorworks

To make the most of the *Colorworks* series it is worthwhile spending some time reading this and the next few pages. *Colorworks* is designed to stimulate a creative use of color. The books do not dictate how color should be applied, but offer advice on how it may be used effectively, giving examples to help generate new ideas. It is essential to remember that *Colorworks* uses the four-color process and that none of the colors or effects use the special brand name ink systems.

The reference system consists of five books that show 125 colors, with 400 type possibilities, 1,000 half-tone options, and 1,500 combinations of color. But even this vast selection should act only as a springboard; the permutations within the books are endless. Use the books as a starting point and experiment!

When choosing colors for graphic design it is almost impossible to predict the finished printed effect. In order to save valuable time spent researching, you can use the series' extensive range of colors to provide references for the shade with which you are working.

The four process colors

Yellow　Magenta　Cyan　Black

▲ Enlarged detail showing how four process colors overlap to produce "realistic" color.

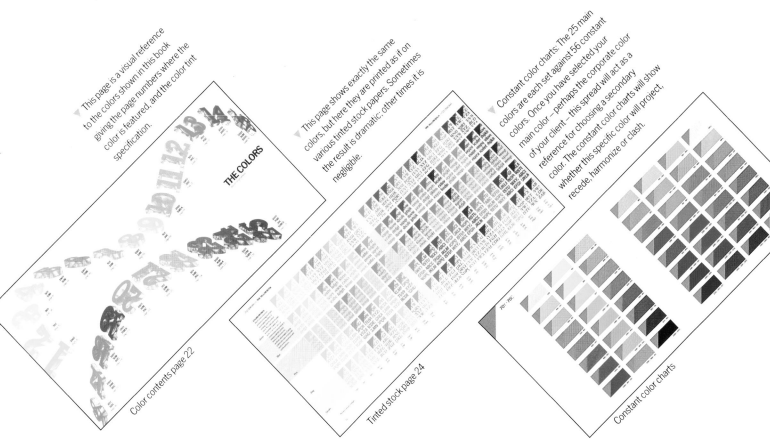

This page is a visual reference to the colors shown in this book giving the page numbers where the color is featured, and the color tint specification.

Color contents page 22

This page shows exactly the same colors, but here they are printed as if on various tinted stock papers. Sometimes the result is dramatic, other times it is negligible.

Tinted stock page 24

Constant color charts: The 25 main colors are each set against 56 constant colors. Once you have selected your main color – perhaps the corporate color of your client – this spread will act as a reference for choosing a secondary color. The constant color charts will show whether this specific color will project, recede, harmonize or clash.

Constant color charts

The books are ideal for showing to clients who are not used to working with color, so that they may see possible results. They will also be particularly useful when working with a specific color, perhaps dictated by a client's company logo, to see how this will combine with other colors. Equally, when working with several colors dictated by circumstances – and perhaps with combinations one is not happy using – you will find that the constant color charts, colorways and applications will show a variety of interesting solutions. The numerous examples in *Colorworks* can act as a catalyst, enabling you to break out of a mental block – a common problem for designers who may feel that they are using a wide variety of colors but actually be working with a small, tight palette.

Finally, when faced with a direct color choice, you should use *Colorworks* in the same way you would use any other art aid – to help create the final image. The books are designed to administer a shot of adrenaline to the design process. They should be treated as a tool and used as a source of both information and inspiration.

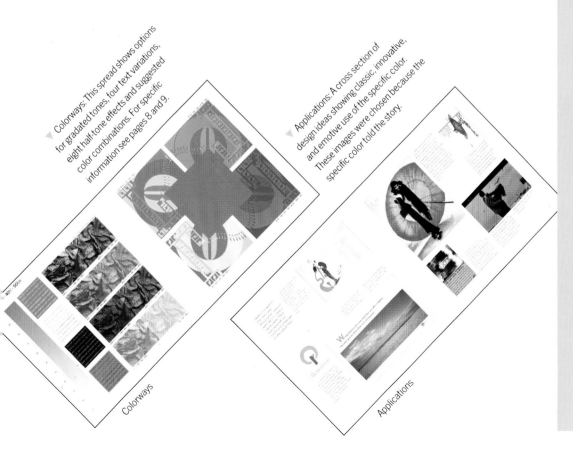

Colorways: This spread shows options for gradated tones, four text variations, eight half-tone effects and suggested color combinations. For specific information see pages 8 and 9.

Applications: A cross section of design ideas showing classic, innovative, and emotive use of the specific color. These images were chosen because the specific color told the story.

Colorways

Applications

TERMINOLOGY USED IN COLORWORKS

Main color: one of the 25 colors featured in each book.

Colorway: The main color plus two other color combinations.

Constant color: The main color with 56 constant colors.

Y: yellow
M: magenta
C: cyan
Blk: black
H/T: half-tone
F/T: flat-tone

TECHNICAL INFORMATION

When using *Colorworks*, or any color specification book, remember that paper stock, lamination and type of ink can change the effect of chosen colors. Coated papers, especially high quality, tend to brighten colors as the ink rests on the surface and the chalk adds extra luminosity, while colors on uncoated paper are absorbed and made duller. Lamination has the effect of making the color darker and richer.

Colorworks specification

Color bar: GRETAG
Screen: 150 L/IN.
Film spec.: AGFA 511P
Tolerance level: +2% −2%
Col. density: C = 1.6 − 1.7
          M = 1.4 − 1.5
          Y = 1.3 − 1.4
          Blk = 1.7 − 1.8
Ink: Proas
Paper: 135gsm matt coated art
Plate spec.: Polychrome
Dot gain: 10%
Printed on: Heidelberg Speedmaster 102v
Printing sequence: Black/Cyan/Magenta/Yellow

On the next four pages you can see, in step-by-step form, exactly how to understand and use the color reference system shown in *Colorworks* and how you can incorporate the ideas into your designs.

It is essential to remember that *Colorworks* uses the four-color process – none of the effects uses the special brand-name ink systems – usually described as "second colors."

1. GRADATED COLOR

The color scale shows the main color fading from full strength to white. If you are using a gradated background, the scale clearly demonstrates at what point reversed-out type would become illegible – with a dark color you may be able to reverse out down to 20% strength, with a pastel only down to 80%, or perhaps not at all, in which case the type should be produced in a dark color.

The opposite would be true if the design incorporated dark type on a fading dark color. Again, unless a very subtle result is required, the scale indicates at what point type would become illegible.

The other use of the fade gives the designer more color options – perhaps you like the color on page 102, but wish it was slightly paler. With the gradated shading you can visualize just how much paler it could be.

2. TYPE OPTIONS

The main color with different type options; solid with white reversed out; type printing in the color; black and the type reversed out as color; solid with black type. These examples demonstrate the problems of size and tonal values of the type.

The type block is made up of two typefaces, a serif and sans serif, both set in two different sizes.

9pt New Baskerville

7pt New Baskerville

Ossidet sterio binignuis gignuntisin stinuand. Flourida

trutent artsquati, quiateire semi uitantque tueri; sol etiam

8½pt Univers 55

7pt Univers 55

Size

Using the four-color process the designer obviously has no problems choosing any combination of tints when using large type, but how small can a specific color type be before it starts to break up or registration becomes a problem? The type block shows when the chosen tints work successfully and more important *when they do not*.

Ossidet sterio binignuis tultia, dolorat isogult it

9pt New Baskerville: 70% Yel demonstrates no problems.

gignuntisin stinuand. Flourida prat gereafiunt quaecumque

7pt New Baskerville 100%Y 70%M 30%C 50% Blk the serifs start to disappear.

Tonal values

Obviously, when dealing with middle ranges of color, printing the type black or reversed out presents no legibility problems. But the critical decisions are where the chosen colors and shade of type are close. Will black type read on dark green? Will white type reverse out of pale pink? When marking up color, it is always easier to play safe, but using the information in *Colorworks* you will be able to take more risks.

Ossidet sterio binignuis tultia, dolorat isogult it

Ossidet sterio binignuis tultia, dolorat isogult it

The problem is shown clearly above: using a pastel color (top) it would be inadvisable to reverse type out; with a middle shade (center) the designer can either reverse out or print in a dark color; while using a dark color (bottom), printing type in black would be illegible (or very subtle).

3. HALF-TONE OPTIONS

This section demonstrates some possibilities of adding color to black and white half-tones where the normal, "realistic" four-color reproduction is not desired or when the originals are black and white prints. This section gives the designer 800 options using various percentages and combinations of the process colors.

100% main color   **50% strength of main color**

100% black H/T plus full strength of the main color

100% black H/T plus 50% of the main color

50% black H/T plus full strength of the main color

50% black H/T plus 50% of the main color

100% black H/T plus a *flat* tint of the main color at full strength

100% black H/T plus a *flat* tint of the main color at half strength

H/T using only the main color at full strength

H/T using only the main color at half strength

Moiré pattern

Some of the main colors in this book include percentages of black. If this film is combined with the black film from the half tone a moiré pattern can occur. To overcome this possibility the films for *Colorworks* have been prepared in two ways. When the main color is made up of 3 colors or less, e.g. p70, the two black films have been specially angled. When the main color is made up of four colors plus the extra black (p140 only) it is impossible to create an extra screen angle. In order to give the effect of the extra black, the repro house has strengthened the black H/T dot in the mid tones and highlights by the appropriate percentage. However, moiré pattern will occur on the flat tint section. Discuss this with your repro house if you want to use B/W half tones with these few colors.

4. COLORWAYS

This page shows the main color with other colors. It acts as a guide to help the designer choose effective color for typography and imagery. Each color is shown as four colorways; each colorway shows the main color with two others.

The three colors in each colorway (corner) are in almost equal proportions. The effect would change dramatically if one color was only a rule or small area. Use the colorways to find the appropriate range for your design and adapt it accordingly.

For information on using the central square and its use in commissioning photography or illustration see page 10.

The choice of color has not been limited to the safe options. The easy neutrals cream, white, and gray have been used, but so have more unusual combinations.

The colors chosen show various effects; look at each corner, if necessary isolating areas.

▼ Colors are shown projecting forward, sometimes using the laws of optics which say that darker, cooler shades recede.

▲ Sometimes, due to the proportions, defying them.

▲ There are classic color combinations.

▲ Colours that are similar in shade.

▲ Use these colors for background patterns, illustrations or typographic designs where the color emphasis has to be equal.

▲ These colors are not advisable if your design needs to highlight a message.

Analyze your design to see how dominant the typography, illustrations, and embellishments need to be versus the background, then use the colorways to pick the appropriate colors or shades.

When selecting colors, it is very important to eliminate any other color elements that might affect your choice. As has been demonstrated in the color optics section (p14), the character of a color can be dramatically changed by other, adjacent colors.

◀ ▲ The colorways have been designed in such a way that you can mask out the other color options – isolating the area you want to work with or even small sections of each design.

▼ ▶ The colorways can also be used if you are selecting the color of typography to match/enhance a photograph or illustration; again masking out the other colorways will help. A print of the photograph or illustration can be positioned in the central area, and the mask moved around.

Useful mask shapes

The design shown on this page was created to demonstrate the practical use of *Colorworks*. It combines many half-tone effects and color combinations.

The options illustrated are drawn from *The Yellow Book*. For more suggestions and further inspiration, refer to the other books in the series.

▶ Using elements from *The Yellow Book* pages 128-29, 130-31.

◄ Using elements from *The Yellow Book* pages 40-41, 42-43.

Yellow introduction

"Any of a group of colours that vary in saturation but have the same hue. They lie in the approximate wavelength range 585-575 nanometres. Yellow is the complementary colour of blue and with cyan and magenta forms a set of primary colours."

Collins English Dictionary; Publishers William Collins Sons and Co. Ltd., London and Glasgow; Second Edition 1986

"Of the color of buttercups and ripe lemons, or of a color approaching this."

Oxford American Dictionary, Publishers Oxford University Press, New York, U.S.A. 1980

Color is not tangible; it is as fluid as a musical note. Although it may be described, the verbal or written words often bear no relation to its actual form. Color has to be seen in context, for a single shade used in conjunction with another color can take on a whole new character. Searching for a particular shade can be very confusing – somewhat like humming a tune and searching for a forgotten note.

No matter how much theory exists, it is the eye of the designer or artist that is responsible for using color creatively. The fact that color can be rationalized and then break its own rules with complete irrationality is what makes it so fascinating.

This book is about process color. By the very nature of the process system, colors are not blended, as with pigments, but shades are selected visually. Unlike pigment colors, process colors can be mixed without losing any of their chromas. The process primary colors are magenta, yellow, and cyan, with black to create density and contrast, allowing dot saturation to establish values of lightness and darkness. The pigment primaries are red, blue and yellow.

The concept of process color is not really new. The German poet and scientist Goethe (1749-1832) looked at effects of light and darkness on pigment color in a way that strongly relates to modern interpretation of process color. In complete contrast, a practical approach was taken by the 20th-century German painter Hickethiev, who created a precise notation system based on cyan, magenta, and yellow for printing. Between these two extremes lies the concept of the process color system.

The colors used in these books had to be systematically chosen to prevent *Colorworks* from dating or the colors from being a purely personal choice. It was important to rely on theory and I finally selected over a thousand colors for the five books that make up this series. This meant working with literally thousands of colors, and yet in spite of this comprehensive palette, there would still be a precise shade that would remain elusive.

*Sunflowers by Vincent van Gogh (1853-90) Yellow is the atmosphere,
the imagery and, through application, the texture.*

My next major task was to select each image from advertising agencies, design consultancies, illustrators, and actually "off the walls." Every piece of printed matter, label, shopping bag or magazine was a potential gold mine of material for the books. Many images had to be excluded, even though they had superb coloration, because they did not tell a story with one predominant color.

Colorworks examples had to have immediate impact, with one color telling the story – whether in harmony with others, through shock tactics, providing a backdrop, creating a period setting, making instant impact for the recognition of the image content, or simply combining superb color use with design.

Color combinations are infinite, and every day wonderful examples of color and design are being created. Having drawn from just some of these, I hope the *Colorworks* series will be a reference to inspire, confirm, and enjoy.

Dale Russell

Optical illusion, proportion, and texture

The painter Wassily Kandinsky described yellow as a lively color which upsets when looked at for a long time and then becomes shrill.

Yellow is the most visible of colors. With its secondaries it attracts attention, and achieves high visibility when teamed with black and white. Lime green and orange can create a fluorescent effect with good visibility.

A bluish-purple is the complementary color of yellow, and these two colors can be used together with great effect. Pink subdues yellow; green is compatible with yellow and adds vitality to it. Next to it orange becomes more brilliant; next to violet it becomes harsh and strong. Red gives yellow dynamism. Lime green can appear crude or common in some contexts, but is currently extremely popular in contemporary design and clothing. It also has good visibility for graphics and packaging.

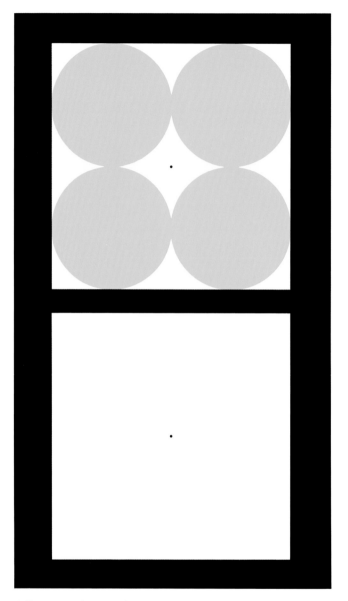

▲ If you stare at the centre of the yellow diagram for 40 seconds and then at the black dot on the white space, the after image created on the white area has violet-blue circles with yellow diamond shapes between. This double interaction of complementary colors was first recognized by Josef Albers and is still of interest to researchers.

▲ The chrome border and the red strip create a sensation of movement which is reinforced by the increase in size of the photographic images.

▲ The page is created with texture and pattern in colors from the same family. The coffee shades, contrasting with yellows and russet have a strongly tactile effect.

▲ The laws of light and color are applied with great effect here. By using black for the first application the designer has allowed the magenta to project, but the greatest impact is reserved for the yellow eye, which appears to shine.

▲▲ This true optical illusion is created by the brightly contrasting yellow on blue. The yellow triangle is "cut out" of the yellow square, revealing a blue triangle – or is it a blue triangle "pasted over" the yellow square?

▲ The stark contrast of black on yellow creates extreme visibility. The use of yellow intensifies the black, which in turn brings clarity to the yellow.

▲ The textured application of ochered tones in varying shades creates an image with depth and contour. This use of hues and intensities, in conjunction with black lines, subtly forms a portrait.

▲ The small red square appears to recede into the yellow background, and yet it acts as a perfect contrast to give visibility to the same shade of red typography.

Psychology

All yellows conjure up nature, from the rich browns of the earth to the golden life-giving rays of the sun and the verdant greens of lush foliage. Hues of yellow create much of the palette of spring, summer, and autumn. If yellow represents the sun, flowers, and fruits, then green is the essence of growth.

The nature of yellow can be completely altered by changing intensities and tones. Whereas the ripe, rich orange of a setting sun dramatically enriches the skyline, the henna tones of the earth can be rich and tactile. A soft, pale yellow is supposed to encourage concentration, and schoolrooms are often painted this color. Chrome yellow exudes a feeling of warmth with almost the same intensity as red, whereas nothing can be more garish than acid yellow or lime green.

Although yellow represents light and energy, it is also associated with sickness, for example, "bile green" and "jaundice yellow." At sea, quarantine is indicated with a yellow flag.

Nature has created a danger warning system based on the combination of yellow and black. Some species of bee, wasp, snake, and frog have black and yellow stripes to warn that they are poisonous. In many parts of the world, humans have adopted this warning signal by printing black on yellow signs for areas where there is poison, toxic fumes, or radiation.

Traffic light systems use green to represent "go", while amber becomes the warning sign – "caution." These colors can produce subliminal reactions if the design refers to this system through color and pattern.

GUESS WHAT'S HERE IN A JIFFY.

▲ By ingeniously relying on the direct psychological association of yellow and lemons it was possible for the designer to adopt a minimalist approach to advertising the product. This has been taken one step further by the confident use of black for the teasing question which assumes that the answer will be "lemon juice."

Guido Bergwitz konzipiert Seminare. Für Pirelli.

PIRELLI
Die Reine Ihres Autos

▲ It is psychologically disturbing to see a bright yellow face. The image has immediate impact and leaves a lasting impression. The yellow tint directly complements the chrome and red logo, giving unity to the entire advertisement.

▲ This immediately recognizable logo has been adopted by many groups and cults from the city of Glasgow to the Acid House cult. The canary yellow with the smiling black graphics is also strongly attractive to young children, representing as it does the sun and happiness.

▲ One immediately becomes aware of the agonies an asthmatic must go through when faced with the terrors of dust. The claustrophobic atmosphere is conveyed by the gray dust coloration of the child and the bed. Although salvation is offered in the text of the brighter facing page, the particular shade of leaf green chosen is still tonally sympathetic with the gray.

▲▲ In this simple design, direct color association has been used to reiterate the sign's message. In many countries amber and black will conjure up the image of a cab, although in this case the black background refers specifically to the British hackney cab.

Official ball of the 1988 French Open.

▲ The use of color manipulates the reaction: the first thing we see is the color – ginger, appropriate for a cat. Next we see the black type on white and read "dog." Result – utter confusion!

▲ Color and graphics combine to transform a plain gray box into a satisfied cat. The yellow type completes the illusion, harmonizing with the coral tongue and bringing warmth to the entire package.

▲ Although the color and texture are immediately recognizable as that of a tennis ball, the shape is that of a croissant. Association through color and form allows the image to evoke both tennis and France.

Marketing

The broad spectrum of yellow encompasses different hues which are popular with all ages and sexes; from the browns, which have a limited appeal when used alone to unconventional shades such as lime and orange which are popular for both direct mail and contemporary graphics.

When used for packaging, yellow blends with orange, brown, and green for various natural and country-style looks. However, yellow with a green hue is a poor choice for food packaging, because it makes one think of mold and rotting food; the same can be said of certain shades of green.

Yellow and green create the atmosphere of sun, forest, sand, and palm trees, enticing the reader to travel. Cream and buttercup yellow evoke dairy products, while the natural ocher shades suggest a healthful diet. Lime, orange, and lemon are the citrus colors, immediately associated with these fruits.

Yellow makes objects look larger and appear to advance toward the consumer and therefore has great impact on the shelf. Combining yellow with colors such as red, royal blue, or black creates a dynamic effect. Pure orange is good for packaging where a dramatic effect is desired.

▲ The evolution of the orange blossom is portrayed through the link between pollination, honey and the bee, using a traditional botanical illustration. A combination of the tones within the illustration reflect the color of the honey. A pure and natural image is created for the buyer who is both selective and health conscious.

▲ Bright orange teamed with teal blue echoes the statement "basic and exciting": the intensity of the orange is given stability by the muted blue. This is for the young and astute, individualistic market.

▲ In this packaging the design concept is that of purity, health, tradition, and ecology. The uncluttered approach implies a guarantee of good value. Shafts of golden light illuminate the cinnamon tones of the packaging, while the use of sienna against pure white for the logo reinforces the message of natural food.

▲ The use of different hues and intensities of brown gives this series of academic books visual continuity. All the shades of brown provide perfect backgrounds for the discreet graphics and, placed together, they form a sophisticated display.

▲ To reinforce the natural qualities of pasta the book jacket uses colors drawn from nature. This theme is reinforced by the textured, undyed paper. The golden yellow of the pasta glows against the pale background and is brought to life by the green herbs.

▲ A distinctive application of bold carmine red typography on a vibrant chrome yellow background, and the delicate use of black for the graphics and calligraphy, form a classic label. The colors chosen are both memorable and clearly visible, while retaining an aura of tradition and high standards that would satisfy the most discerning of shoppers.

▲ ▲ The orange typography clashes with the red logo and stands out boldly against the blue background. This is dynamic marketing accurately aimed at a specialist sector.

▲ This readily evokes images of shopping for groceries in local markets on foreign trips. The ripe, sensuous yellow of the pepper and the glass of red wine, with its matching border, will appeal to the discerning shopper.

Culture and period

Throughout the Christian world, yellow is synonymous with Easter, which falls in spring in the northern hemisphere – a time of new life. Yellow was used in the backgrounds of religious paintings by early masters to represent the kingdom of sun and light. It is symbolic of a hidden truth and the glory of Christ's resurrection. Conversely, however, Judas was often depicted wearing a yellow coat.

In some eastern religions yellow is a sacred color – Buddhist monks wear saffron robes, and in China the emperor is associated with yellow. However, in a totally different context, "yellow books" in China are pornographic ones – a usage similar to that of "blue" in the West. In Pakistan, yellow and black represent hell. Orange should be used with caution in the Republic of Ireland, where it has strong associations with the Protestant religion and the Orangemen.

In the United States, a yellow ribbon was traditionally worn by the women waiting for their men to come home from the cavalry during the late 19th century. The ribbon represented the yellow neckerchiefs worn by the soldiers. Conversely in 1876 American women wore yellow ribbons as a sign of their struggle for women's rights. In English-speaking countries, the expression "follow the yellow brick road" from the book and film *The Wizard of Oz* has overtones of a hopeful journey.

▲ Egyptian hieroglyphics are given authenticity by the color palette of natural pigments used for wall painting in early Egypt. It is only a second glance that makes one aware of the anachronism.

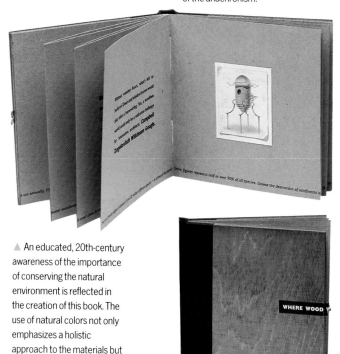

▲ An educated, 20th-century awareness of the importance of conserving the natural environment is reflected in the creation of this book. The use of natural colors not only emphasizes a holistic approach to the materials but also complements the ecological message.

▲ ▲ The exotic flavor of this dust jacket is intensified by the overall use of yellow and orange tones, combined with green. Color and graphics unite to bring a pre-historic culture to life.

▲ The 1940s image is retained in the updated graphics for the packaging of these French cigarettes. Traditionally Gauloises have always had a blue and white pack so the introduction of yellow is immediately noticeable. Even for those who have not seen the original pack, the yellow headlights have instant impact.

▲ The color and graphics here are immediately evocative of the early 1950s. The use of mustard with black and minimal amounts of red dates the illustration.

▲ ▲ Everything in this image conspires to create a strong impression of the late Victorian period. Shades of orange, brown, and black evoke an impression of age, asserting that this beer is the original product, unspoiled by time. This atmosphere is reinforced by applying the image to tiles.

▲ Femininity and desirability are romantically portrayed on this box for a floral toilet water which echoes the sepia tones of early 20th-century design. The seductive pink tones are cocooned by soft shades of brown, while the introduction of gold conveys the idea of excellence.

▲ Cadmium yellow, combined with magenta, red, and turquoise, creates a discordant palette, punctuated by gray, black, and blue. This daring use of color is typical of that found in the experimental youth culture graphics of independent publications in the late 1980s.

**70Y
10C**
page 64

**100Y
30BLK**
page 68

**100Y
30C**
page 72

**50Y
50C**
page 78

**70Y
70C**
page 82

**100Y
100C**
page 86

**100Y
30M
100C**
page 90

THE COLORS

Numbers are percentages

**80Y
30M
20C**
page 124

**100Y
40M
50BLK**
page 128

**100Y
70M
50BLK**
page 134

**100Y
70M
30C
50BLK**
page 138

COLORS ON TINTS

The 25 main colors are printed on background tints to simulate the effect of printing color on printed stock. This chart can be used in a number of ways: as a guide to see how pale your chosen color can go before it merges with the printed stock; to determine the aesthetic advantages of using a particular color on a specific stock and to experiment with subtle patterns.

The corner flashes (triangles) show the main color in its pure state, while the lettering shows the color printed on the tint.

Green

Blue

Pink

Gray

Cream

100Y	70Y	50Y	50Y 10M	100Y 30M	100Y 50M	70Y 30M	100Y 10M	70Y 10C	100Y 30BLK	100Y 30C

Numbers are percentages

| 50Y 50C | 70Y 70C | 100Y 100C | 100Y 30M 100C | 80Y 60C | 100Y 30M 50C | 100Y 30M 60C | 100Y 70BLK | 100Y 30M 30C | 70Y 30M 30C | 80Y 30M 20C | 100Y 40M 50BLK | 100Y 70M 50BLK | 100Y 70M 30C 50BLK |

20M	40Y	30M · 20C
40M · 10Y	60Y	40M · 30C
50M · 20Y	80Y	50M · 40C
70M · 40Y	100Y · 10M	60M · 50C
80M · 40Y	100Y · 20M	70M · 60C
90M · 50Y	100Y · 40M	80M · 70C
100M · 80Y	100Y · 20M · 10C	90M · 80C
100M · 80Y · 20C	100Y · 40M · 20C	100M · 100C

40C	20C • 50Y	60Y • 30M	10Blk
60C	40C • 100Y	70Y • 50M	30Blk
80C • 10M	50C • 80Y	70Y • 80M	50Blk • 10Y
100C • 30M	80C • 100Y • 10M	90Y • 70M • 10C	50Blk • 10M
90C • 40M	100C • 80Y • 10M	90Y • 70M • 30C	70Blk
100C • 50M • 10Y	100C • 100Y • 40M	90Y • 80M • 40C	70Blk • 30C
100C • 60M	100C • 100Y • 60M	100Y • 90M • 50C	80Blk
100C • 80M • 10Y	100C • 100Y • 80M	100Y • 100M • 80C	100Blk

NOTE: For technical information see page 6

100
90
80
70
60
50
40
30
20
10
0

Ossidet sterio binignuis tultia, dolorat isogult it gignuntisin stinuand. Flourida prat gereafiunt quaecumque trutent artsquati, quiateire lurorist de corspore orum semi uitantque tueri; sol etiam caecat contra osidetsal utiquite

Ossidet sterio binignuis tultia, dolorat isogult it gignuntisin stinuand. Flourida prat gereafiunt quaecumque trutent artsquati, quiateire lurorist de corspore orum semi uitantque tueri; sol etiam caecat contra osidetsal utiquite

Ossidet sterio binignuis tultia, dolorat isogult it gignuntisin stinuand. Flourida prat gereafiunt quaecumque trutent artsquati, quiateire lurorist de corspore orum semi uitantque tueri; sol etiam caecat contra osidetsal utiquite

Ossidet sterio binignuis tultia, dolorat isogult it gignuntisin stinuand. Flourida prat gereafiunt quaecumque trutent artsquati, quiateire lurorist de corspore orum semi uitantque tueri; sol etiam caecat contra osidetsal utiquite

100Blk H/T • H/T's: **100**Y   100Blk H/T • H/T's: **50**Y

50Blk H/T • H/T's: **100**Y   50Blk H/T • H/T's: **50**Y

100Blk H/T • F/T's: **100**Y   100Blk H/T • F/T's: **50**Y

H/T's: **100**Y   H/T's: **50**Y

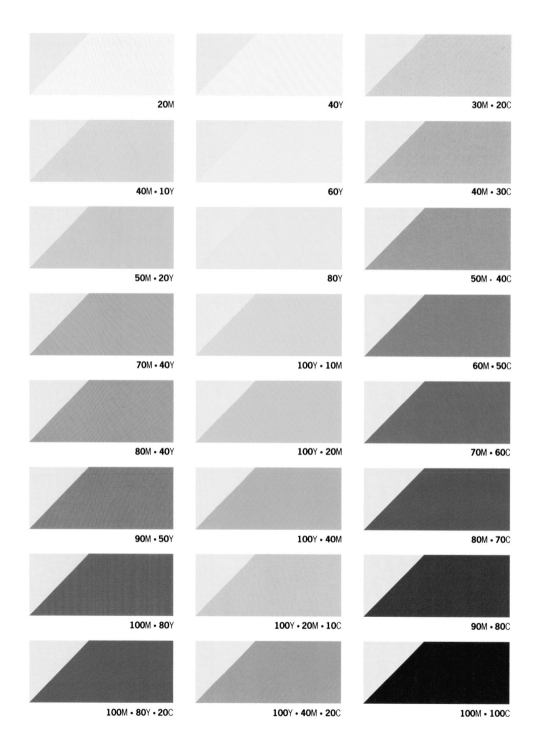

20M

40Y

30M · 20C

40M · 10Y

60Y

40M · 30C

50M · 20Y

80Y

50M · 40C

70M · 40Y

100Y · 10M

60M · 50C

80M · 40Y

100Y · 20M

70M · 60C

90M · 50Y

100Y · 40M

80M · 70C

100M · 80Y

100Y · 20M · 10C

90M · 80C

100M · 80Y · 20C

100Y · 40M · 20C

100M · 100C

40C	20C · 50Y	60Y · 30M	10Blk
60C	40C · 100Y	70Y · 50M	30Blk
80C · 10M	50C · 80Y	70Y · 80M	50Blk · 10Y
100C · 30M	80C · 100Y · 10M	90Y · 70M · 10C	50Blk · 10M
90C · 40M	100C · 80Y · 10M	90Y · 70M · 30C	70Blk
100C · 50M · 10Y	100C · 100Y · 40M	90Y · 80M · 40C	70Blk · 30C
100C · 60M	100C · 100Y · 60M	100Y · 90M · 50C	80Blk
100C · 80M · 10Y	100C · 100Y · 80M	100Y · 100M · 80C	100Blk

NOTE: For technical information see page 6

Ossidet sterio binignuis tultia, dolorat isogult it gignuntisin stinuand. Flourida prat gereafiunt quaecumque trutent artsquati, quiateire lurorist de corspore orum semi uitantque tueri; sol etiam caecat contra osidetsal utiquite

Ossidet sterio binignuis tultia, dolorat isogult it gignuntisin stinuand. Flourida prat gereafiunt quaecumque trutent artsquati, quiateire lurorist de corspore orum semi uitantque tueri; sol etiam caecat contra osidetsal utiquite

Ossidet sterio binignuis tultia, dolorat isogult it gignuntisin stinuand. Flourida prat gereafiunt quaecumque trutent artsquati, quiateire lurorist de corspore orum semi uitantque tueri; sol etiam caecat contra osidetsal utiquite

Ossidet sterio binignuis tultia, dolorat isogult it gignuntisin stinuand. Flourida prat gereafiunt quaecumque trutent artsquati, quiateire lurorist de corspore orum semi uitantque tueri; sol etiam caecat contra osidetsal utiquite

100 Blk H/T • H/T's: **70**Y   **100**Blk H/T • H/T's: **35**Y

50Blk H/T • H/T's:**70**Y   **50**Blk H/T • H/T's: **35**Y

100 Blk H/T • F/T's: **70**Y   **100**Blk H/T • F/T's: **35**Y

H/T's: **70**Y   H/T's: **35**Y

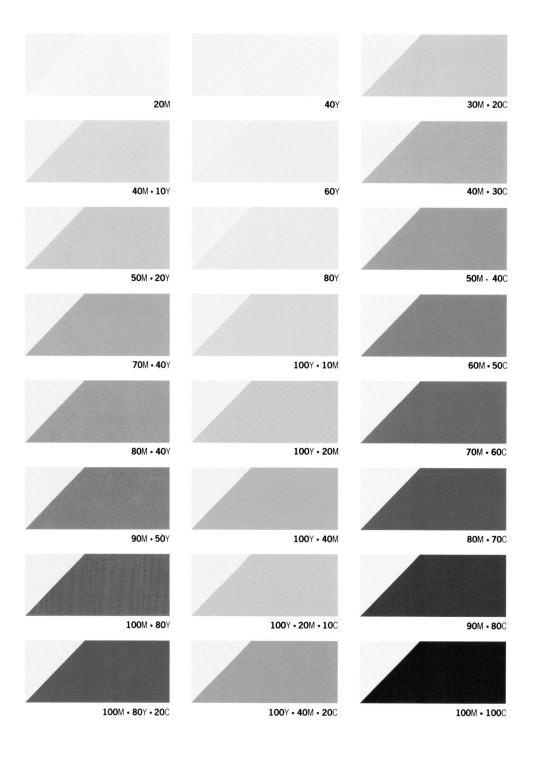

20M

40Y

30M · 20C

40M · 10Y

60Y

40M · 30C

50M · 20Y

80Y

50M · 40C

70M · 40Y

100Y · 10M

60M · 50C

80M · 40Y

100Y · 20M

70M · 60C

90M · 50Y

100Y · 40M

80M · 70C

100M · 80Y

100Y · 20M · 10C

90M · 80C

100M · 80Y · 20C

100Y · 40M · 20C

100M · 100C

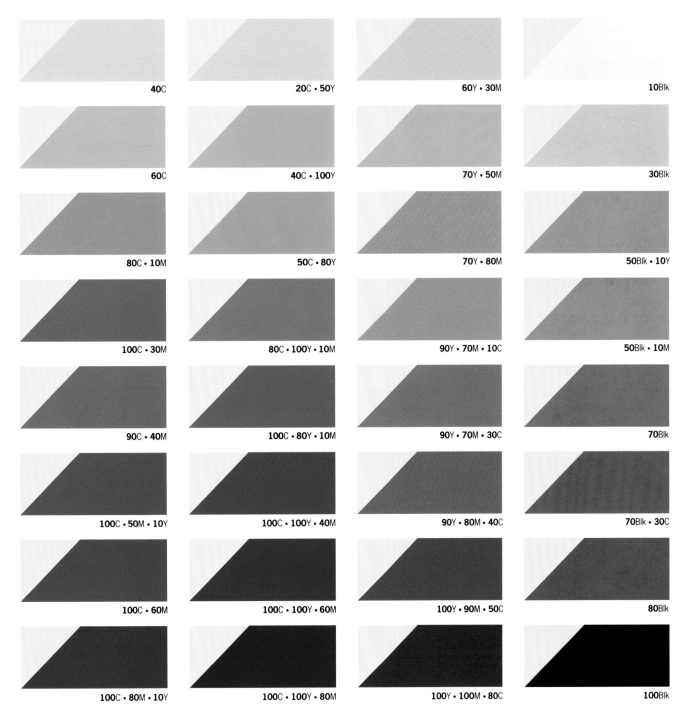

40C	20C • 50Y	60Y • 30M	10Blk
60C	40C • 100Y	70Y • 50M	30Blk
80C • 10M	50C • 80Y	70Y • 80M	50Blk • 10Y
100C • 30M	80C • 100Y • 10M	90Y • 70M • 10C	50Blk • 10M
90C • 40M	100C • 80Y • 10M	90Y • 70M • 30C	70Blk
100C • 50M • 10Y	100C • 100Y • 40M	90Y • 80M • 40C	70Blk • 30C
100C • 60M	100C • 100Y • 60M	100Y • 90M • 50C	80Blk
100C • 80M • 10Y	100C • 100Y • 80M	100Y • 100M • 80C	100Blk

50Y

NOTE: For technical information see page 6

100

90

80

Ossidet sterio binignuis tultia, dolorat isogult it gignuntisin stinuand. Flourida prat gereafiunt quaecumque trutent artsquati, quiateire lurorist de corspore orum semi uitantque tueri; sol etiam caecat contra osidetsal utiquite

100 Blk H/T • H/T's: **50**Y

100 Blk H/T • H/T's: **25**Y

70

60

Ossidet sterio binignuis tultia, dolorat isogult it gignuntisin stinuand. Flourida prat gereafiunt quaecumque trutent artsquati, quiateire lurorist de corspore orum semi uitantque tueri; sol etiam caecat contra osidetsal utiquite

50Blk H/T • H/T's: **50**Y

50Blk H/T • H/T's: **25**Y

50

Ossidet sterio binignuis tultia, dolorat isogult it gignuntisin stinuand. Flourida prat gereafiunt quaecumque trutent artsquati, quiateire lurorist de corspore orum semi uitantque tueri; sol etiam caecat contra osidetsal utiquite

40

30

100 Blk H/T • F/T's: **50**Y

100 Blk H/T • F/T's: **25**Y

20

Ossidet sterio binignuis tultia, dolorat isogult it gignuntisin stinuand. Flourida prat gereafiunt quaecumque trutent artsquati, quiateire lurorist de corspore orum semi uitantque tueri; sol etiam caecat contra osidetsal utiquite

10

0

H/T's: **50**Y

H/T's: **25**Y

A luminous yellow, a yellow of activity - fluorescent, positive, and electric. It attracts fellow pigment primaries - red and blue - but counters the process primaries, magenta and cyan.

IL MISANTROPO

CASSA DI RISPARMIO DI ROMA
Cultura viva dalla tua amica banca.

◀ This image is created by the use of simple graphics and a strong, unconventional color palette. The three-dimensional effect is achieved in two ways: the application of colors in three layers, and the creation of an optical illusion by placing a complementary process yellow onto royal blue above a tonal shade of teal. The white type projects from the teal background.

▼ This anarchic approach to color reflects the chaotic modernist graphics as well as the subject of the book. The disharmony of brash process yellow against soft peach and Wedgewood blue is bridged by the scattered touches of *café au lait* interplaying with the white-on-black graphics. The yellow banner also serves to highlight the title.

▲ Simple geometric shapes and typeface in black and process yellow form a sophisticated image when applied to terra cotta. Juxtaposed with the subtle, muted tones of terra cotta, this aggressive shade of yellow becomes surprisingly warm.

◀ Primary yellow makes an effective background for the associated symbols of blue for water and green for mountain foliage. The yellow not only provides a continuity of packaging but also has a practical purpose, as it is highly visible in an emergency.

◀ Process yellow forms a blatant background while the subtlest of violet graphics brings texture to the book cover. Demarcation of areas within a narrow border provides visual stimulation through the interplay between tones of sepia yellow and violet. In this instance the roles are reversed and violet becomes dominant. The tantalizing glimpse of graphics relates to the black type on the taupe and sepia tints.

▲ Process yellow lettering attracts attention and, combined with grass green, creates a clean, fresh impression. The yellow strengthens the green without swamping the black cat graphics.

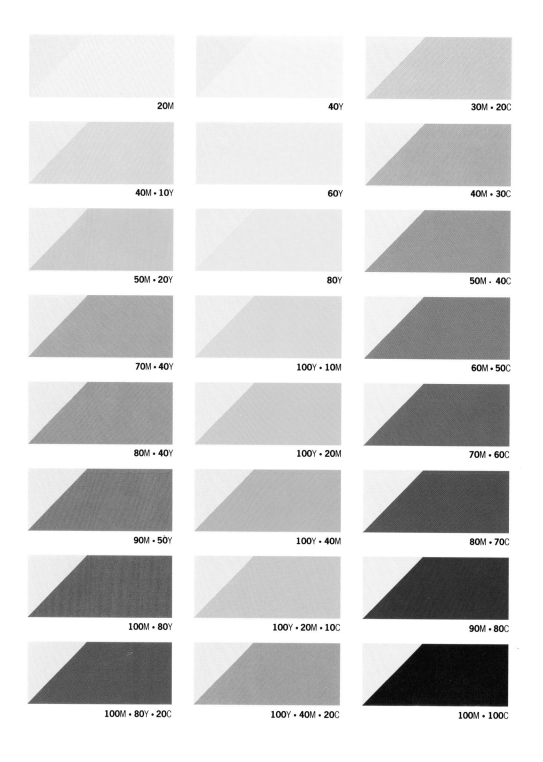

20M

40Y

30M · 20C

40M · 10Y

60Y

40M · 30C

50M · 20Y

80Y

50M · 40C

70M · 40Y

100Y · 10M

60M · 50C

80M · 40Y

100Y · 20M

70M · 60C

90M · 50Y

100Y · 40M

80M · 70C

100M · 80Y

100Y · 20M · 10C

90M · 80C

100M · 80Y · 20C

100Y · 40M · 20C

100M · 100C

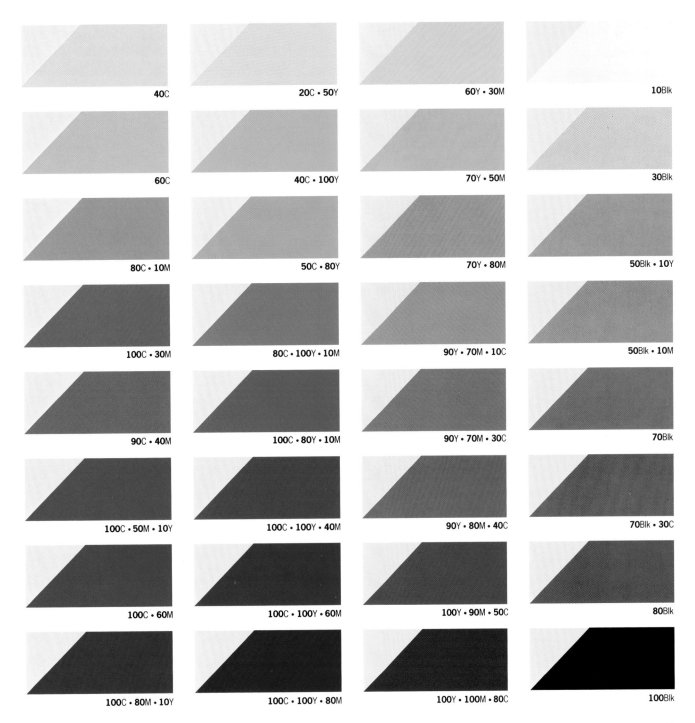

40C

20C • 50Y

60Y • 30M

10Blk

60C

40C • 100Y

70Y • 50M

30Blk

80C • 10M

50C • 80Y

70Y • 80M

50Blk • 10Y

100C • 30M

80C • 100Y • 10M

90Y • 70M • 10C

50Blk • 10M

90C • 40M

100C • 80Y • 10M

90Y • 70M • 30C

70Blk

100C • 50M • 10Y

100C • 100Y • 40M

90Y • 80M • 40C

70Blk • 30C

100C • 60M

100C • 100Y • 60M

100Y • 90M • 50C

80Blk

100C • 80M • 10Y

100C • 100Y • 80M

100Y • 100M • 80C

100Blk

100
90
80
70
60
50
40
30
20
10
0

Ossidet sterio binignuis
tultia, dolorat isogult it
gignuntisin stinuand. Flourida
prat gereafiunt quaecumque
trutent artsquati, quiateire
lurorist de corspore orum
semi uitantque tueri; sol etiam
caecat contra osidetsal utiquite

Ossidet sterio binignuis
tultia, dolorat isogult it
gignuntisin stinuand. Flourida
prat gereafiunt quaecumque
trutent artsquati, quiateire
lurorist de corspore orum
semi uitantque tueri; sol etiam
caecat contra osidetsal utiquite

Ossidet sterio binignuis
tultia, dolorat isogult it
gignuntisin stinuand. Flourida
prat gereafiunt quaecumque
trutent artsquati, quiateire
lurorist de corspore orum
semi uitantque tueri; sol etiam
caecat contra osidetsal utiquite

Ossidet sterio binignuis
tultia, dolorat isogult it
gignuntisin stinuand. Flourida
prat gereafiunt quaecumque
trutent artsquati, quiateire
lurorist de corspore orum
semi uitantque tueri; sol etiam
caecat contra osidetsal utiquite

NOTE: For technical information see page 6

100Blk H/T • H/T's: **50**Y • **10**M   100Blk H/T • H/T's: **25**Y • **5**M

50Blk H/T • H/T's: **50**Y • **10**M   50Blk H/T • H/T's: **25**Y • **5**M

100Blk H/T • F/T's: **50**Y • **10**M   100Blk H/T • F/T's: **25**Y • **5**M

H/T's: **50**Y • **10**M   H/T's: **25**Y • **5**M

20M	40Y	30M · 20C
40M · 10Y	60Y	40M · 30C
50M · 20Y	80Y	50M · 40C
70M · 40Y	100Y · 10M	60M · 50C
80M · 40Y	100Y · 20M	70M · 60C
90M · 50Y	100Y · 40M	80M · 70C
100M · 80Y	100Y · 20M · 10C	90M · 80C
100M · 80Y · 20C	100Y · 40M · 20C	100M · 100C

40C

20C • 50Y

60Y • 30M

10Blk

60C

40C • 100Y

70Y • 50M

30Blk

80C • 10M

50C • 80Y

70Y • 80M

50Blk • 10Y

100C • 30M

80C • 100Y • 10M

90Y • 70M • 10C

50Blk • 10M

90C • 40M

100C • 80Y • 10M

90Y • 70M • 30C

70Blk

100C • 50M • 10Y

100C • 100Y • 40M

90Y • 80M • 40C

70Blk • 30C

100C • 60M

100C • 100Y • 60M

100Y • 90M • 50C

80Blk

100C • 80M • 10Y

100C • 100Y • 80M

100Y • 100M • 80C

100Blk

NOTE: For technical information see page 6

100

90

80

Ossidet sterio binignuis tultia, dolorat isogult it gignuntisin stinuand. Flourida prat gereafiunt quaecumque trutent artsquati, quiateire lurorist de corspore orum semi uitantque tueri; sol etiam caecat contra osidetsal utiquite

10Blk H/T • H/T's: **100**Y · **30**M   100Blk H/T • H/T's: **50**Y · **15**M

70

60

Ossidet sterio binignuis tultia, dolorat isogult it gignuntisin stinuand. Flourida prat gereafiunt quaecumque trutent artsquati, quiateire lurorist de corspore orum semi uitantque tueri; sol etiam caecat contra osidetsal utiquite

50Blk H/T • H/T's: **100**Y · **30**M   50Blk H/T • H/T's: **50**Y · **15**M

50

40

Ossidet sterio binignuis tultia, dolorat isogult it gignuntisin stinuand. Flourida prat gereafiunt quaecumque trutent artsquati, quiateire lurorist de corspore orum semi uitantque tueri; sol etiam caecat contra osidetsal utiquite

100Blk H/T • F/T's: **100**Y · **30**M   100Blk H/T • F/T's: **50**Y · **15**M

30

20

Ossidet sterio binignuis tultia, dolorat isogult it gignuntisin stinuand. Flourida prat gereafiunt quaecumque trutent artsquati, quiateire lurorist de corspore orum semi uitantque tueri; sol etiam caecat contra osidetsal utiquite

10

0

H/T's: **100**Y · **30**M   H/T's: **50**Y · **15**M

■ **70**Y • **100**M ■ **30**M • **80**C • **20**Blk

■ **50**M • **20**C • **10**Blk ■ **20**Y • **70**C

■ **10**Y • **10**Blk ■ **20**C • **10**Blk

■ **20**Y • **40**C • **30**Blk ■ **10**Y • **100**M • **40**C • **20**Blk

20M

40Y

30M · 20C

40M · 10Y

60Y

40M · 30C

50M · 20Y

80Y

50M · 40C

70M · 40Y

100Y · 10M

60M · 50C

80M · 40Y

100Y · 20M

70M · 60C

90M · 50Y

100Y · 40M

80M · 70C

100M · 80Y

100Y · 20M · 10C

90M · 80C

100M · 80Y · 20C

100Y · 40M · 20C

100M · 100C

40C	20C · 50Y	60Y · 30M	10Blk
60C	40C · 100Y	70Y · 50M	30Blk
80C · 10M	50C · 80Y	70Y · 80M	50Blk · 10Y
100C · 30M	80C · 100Y · 10M	90Y · 70M · 10C	50Blk · 10M
90C · 40M	100C · 80Y · 10M	90Y · 70M · 30C	70Blk
100C · 50M · 10Y	100C · 100Y · 40M	90Y · 80M · 40C	70Blk · 30C
100C · 60M	100C · 100Y · 60M	100Y · 90M · 50C	80Blk
100C · 80M · 10Y	100C · 100Y · 80M	100Y · 100M · 80C	100Blk

49

100Y · 50M

NOTE: For technical information see page 6

100

90

80

70

60

50

40

30

20

10

0

Ossidet sterio binignuis tultia, dolorat isogult it gignuntisin stinuand. Flourida prat gereafiunt quaecumque **trutent artsquati, quiateire lurorist de corspore orum** semi uitantque tueri; sol etiam caecat contra osidetsal utiquite

Ossidet sterio binignuis tultia, dolorat isogult it gignuntisin stinuand. Flourida prat gereafiunt quaecumque **trutent artsquati, quiateire lurorist de corspore orum** semi uitantque tueri; sol etiam caecat contra osidetsal utiquite

Ossidet sterio binignuis tultia, dolorat isogult it gignuntisin stinuand. Flourida prat gereafiunt quaecumque **trutent artsquati, quiateire lurorist de corspore orum** semi uitantque tueri; sol etiam caecat contra osidetsal utiquite

Ossidet sterio binignuis tultia, dolorat isogult it gignuntisin stinuand. Flourida prat gereafiunt quaecumque **trutent artsquati, quiateire lurorist de corspore orum** semi uitantque tueri; sol etiam caecat contra osidetsal utiquite

100 Blk H/T • H/T's: **100**Y • **50**M   **100**Blk H/T • H/T's: **50**Y • **25**M

50Blk H/T • H/T's: **100**Y • **50**M   **50**Blk H/T • H/T's: **50**Y • **25**M

100 Blk H/T • F/T's: **100**Y • **50**M   **100**Blk H/T • F/T's: **50**Y • **25**M

H/T's: **100**Y • **50**M   H/T's: **50**Y • **25**M

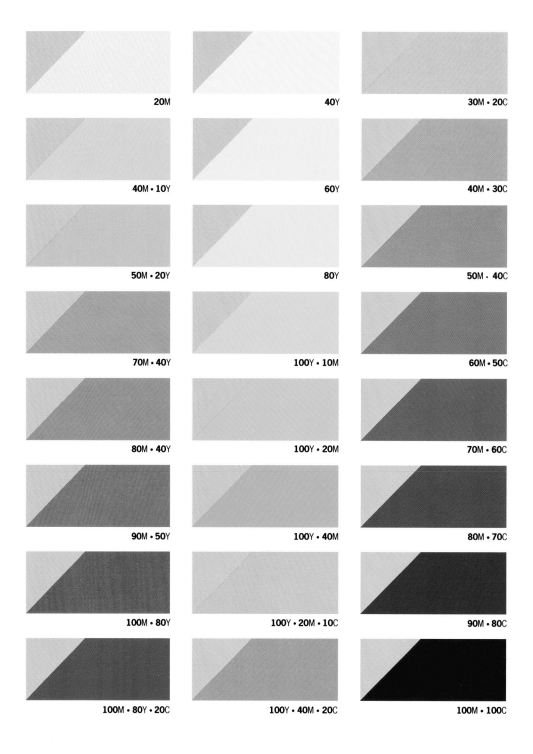

20M

40Y

30M · 20C

40M · 10Y

60Y

40M · 30C

50M · 20Y

80Y

50M · 40C

70M · 40Y

100Y · 10M

60M · 50C

80M · 40Y

100Y · 20M

70M · 60C

90M · 50Y

100Y · 40M

80M · 70C

100M · 80Y

100Y · 20M · 10C

90M · 80C

100M · 80Y · 20C

100Y · 40M · 20C

100M · 100C

40C	20C • 50Y	60Y • 30M	10Blk
60C	40C • 100Y	70Y • 50M	30Blk
80C • 10M	50C • 80Y	70Y • 80M	50Blk • 10Y
100C • 30M	80C • 100Y • 10M	90Y • 70M • 10C	50Blk • 10M
90C • 40M	100C • 80Y • 10M	90Y • 70M • 30C	70Blk
100C • 50M • 10Y	100C • 100Y • 40M	90Y • 80M • 40C	70Blk • 30C
100C • 60M	100C • 100Y • 60M	100Y • 90M • 50C	80Blk
100C • 80M • 10Y	100C • 100Y • 80M	100Y • 100M • 80C	100Blk

100

90

80

70

60

50

40

30

20

10

0

NOTE: For technical information see page 6

Ossidet sterio binignuis tultia, dolorat isogult it gignuntisin stinuand. Flourida prat gereafiunt quaecumque trutent artsquati, quiateire lurorist de corspore orum semi uitantque tueri; sol etiam caecat contra osidetsal utiquite

Ossidet sterio binignuis tultia, dolorat isogult it gignuntisin stinuand. Flourida prat gereafiunt quaecumque trutent artsquati, quiateire lurorist de corspore orum semi uitantque tueri; sol etiam caecat contra osidetsal utiquite

Ossidet sterio binignuis tultia, dolorat isogult it gignuntisin stinuand. Flourida prat gereafiunt quaecumque trutent artsquati, quiateire lurorist de corspore orum semi uitantque tueri; sol etiam caecat contra osidetsal utiquite

Ossidet sterio binignuis tultia, dolorat isogult it gignuntisin stinuand. Flourida prat gereafiunt quaecumque trutent artsquati, quiateire lurorist de corspore orum semi uitantque tueri; sol etiam caecat contra osidetsal utiquite

100Blk H/T • H/T's: **70**Y • **30**M   100Blk H/T • H/T's: **35**Y • **15**M

50Blk H/T • H/T's: **70**Y • **30**M   50Blk H/T • H/T's: **35**Y • **15**M

100Blk H/T • F/T's: **70**Y • **30**M   100Blk H/T • F/T's: **35**Y • **15**M

H/T's: **70**Y • **30**M   H/T's: **35**Y • **15**M

Shades of a sunburst, from ripe orange through golden yellow to palest apricot, create a natural palette. These tones blend with one another and complement all other natural tones.

▶ The flowing movement of the ocher and black illustration is picked up in the formal typography of the documentation. Using this ochered yellow for the headings breaks the consistency of the black type in this brave deviation from the standard company report.

▲ A round tree in its simplest form becomes the Rowntree candy logo. It is given childlike abstraction with a complex color composition. Golden yellow teamed with rich brown reproduces the coloring of nature, confirming the image of the logo. These strong shades perform the task of primary colors without the brashness.

▼ The expansive golden fields and wide blue skies provide the story behind the caption, further emphasized by the Indian yellow of the dropped capital in the typography. The rich saffron shades reinforce the connotations of abundance in a ripe golden harvest.

Shades of burnt orange and golden yellow filter through the parasol, producing a glowing backdrop to the classic 1920s figure. The orientally inspired style and posture reinforce the symbolic sun shape of the glowing parasol. The haze from the orange and yellow absorbs the flesh tones and softens the black to create an indistinct finish. Set against a wash of pale blue, the sunshade becomes the dominant object, while the eye is drawn to the central black-draped figure.

A complex diagram in an academic book forms part of an overall graphic design which relies on a subtle and discreet use of color for its effectiveness. The grayed lilac of the illustration and the minimal black graphics are given warmth and interest by the mandarin yellow.

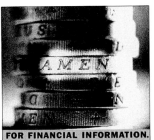

**FOR FINANCIAL INFORMATION.
THE LAST WORD IN DETAIL.**

Information. You want it. Detailed, concise and before anyone else. Financial Times Newsletters have it. A regularly updated picture of world finance in pin-sharp focus. Hard facts from international sources, illuminated by our top analysts and commentators. This is the information that gives you the edge. *ftbi*

The wealth of gold is the overpowering statement in this dominantly yellow advertisement. The rich saffron background behind the text allows the softer gold shades of the coins to glow gently in shafts of white light. This rich shade of yellow also gives clarity to the black typography and enhances visibility.

The use of a sienna tint for this highly evocative photograph not only creates the atmosphere of a sybaritic late afternoon picnic but also echoes the color of cognac. The warmth of this shade is underlined by red, while the discreet black background projects the white typography and reinforces the image of adult sophistication.

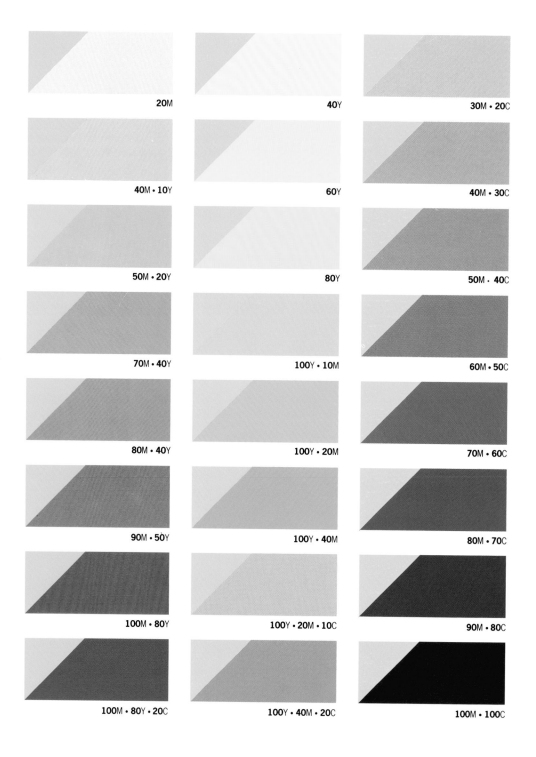

20M

40Y

30M · 20C

40M · 10Y

60Y

40M · 30C

50M · 20Y

80Y

50M · 40C

70M · 40Y

100Y · 10M

60M · 50C

80M · 40Y

100Y · 20M

70M · 60C

90M · 50Y

100Y · 40M

80M · 70C

100M · 80Y

100Y · 20M · 10C

90M · 80C

100M · 80Y · 20C

100Y · 40M · 20C

100M · 100C

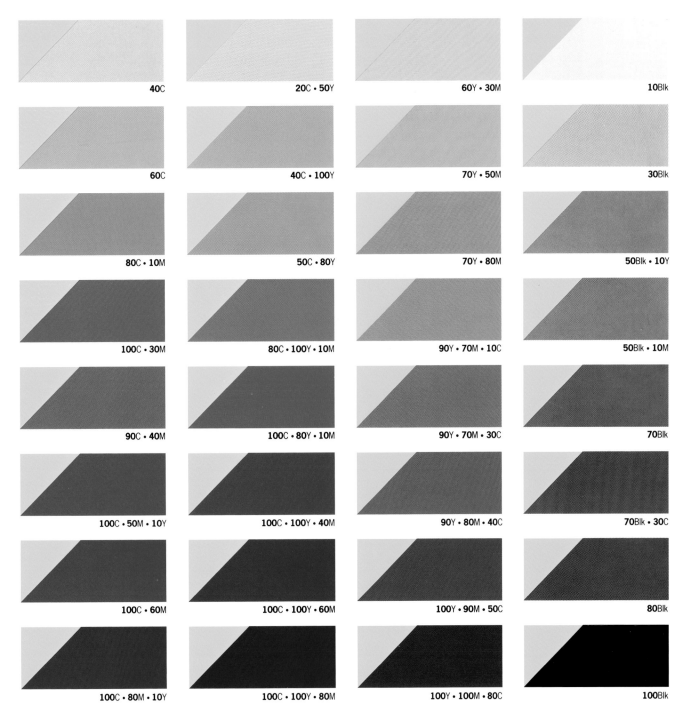

40C

20C • 50Y

60Y • 30M

10Blk

60C

40C • 100Y

70Y • 50M

30Blk

80C • 10M

50C • 80Y

70Y • 80M

50Blk • 10Y

100C • 30M

80C • 100Y • 10M

90Y • 70M • 10C

50Blk • 10M

90C • 40M

100C • 80Y • 10M

90Y • 70M • 30C

70Blk

100C • 50M • 10Y

100C • 100Y • 40M

90Y • 80M • 40C

70Blk • 30C

100C • 60M

100C • 100Y • 60M

100Y • 90M • 50C

80Blk

100C • 80M • 10Y

100C • 100Y • 80M

100Y • 100M • 80C

100Blk

100Y · 10M

NOTE: For technical information see page 6

Ossidet sterio binignuis
tultia, dolorat isogult it
gignuntisin stinuand. Flourida
prat gereafiunt quaecumque
trutent artsquati, quiateire
lurorist de corspore orum
semi uitantque tueri; sol etiam
caecat contra osidetsal utiquite

100Blk H/T · H/T's: **100**Y · **10**M   100Blk H/T · H/T's: **50**Y · **5**M

Ossidet sterio binignuis
tultia, dolorat isogult it
gignuntisin stinuand. Flourida
prat gereafiunt quaecumque
trutent artsquati, quiateire
lurorist de corspore orum
semi uitantque tueri; sol etiam
caecat contra osidetsal utiquite

50Blk H/T · H/T's: **100**Y · **10**M   50Blk H/T · H/T's: **50**Y · **5**M

Ossidet sterio binignuis
tultia, dolorat isogult it
gignuntisin stinuand. Flourida
prat gereafiunt quaecumque
trutent artsquati, quiateire
lurorist de corspore orum
semi uitantque tueri; sol etiam
caecat contra osidetsal utiquite

100Blk H/T · F/T's: **100**Y · **10**M   100Blk H/T · F/T's: **50**Y · **5**M

Ossidet sterio binignuis
tultia, dolorat isogult it
gignuntisin stinuand. Flourida
prat gereafiunt quaecumque
trutent artsquati, quiateire
lurorist de corspore orum
semi uitantque tueri; sol etiam
caecat contra osidetsal utiquite

H/T's: **100**Y · **10**M   H/T's: **50**Y · **5**M

Sunflowers, fields of wheat, and hot summer days are evoked by the simplest and yet most powerful of yellows. This highly visible, rich, warm chrome complements other shades.

▷ Corporate identity and continuity are developed through the typography of these three brochures. The colors have an alert, pure style, using a role-reversal of hue. Powder blue on sunflower yellow has a jarring effect when used in this way, as the more obvious application would be yellow on blue.

◁ Strong shades of chrome yellow and leaf green form the basis for a company logo aimed at parents and children. The teaming of yellow and green has a natural association with the growth of plants, which relates in turn to growing children and the need for new shoes. The green background projects the rich yellow typography, giving visibility while creating a friendly, young image. The extreme simplicity of the design allows the colors to tell the story.

▷ An imaginative color palette is adapted to create a positive company identity which is both memorable and distinctive, without losing aesthetic appeal. Chrome yellow is the most visible of all the colors and has been appropriately applied to dominate wherever it is positioned within the designs. The chrome and terra cotta tonally complement each other while contrasting against the soft black, while *eau-de-nil* is used as an additional highlight.

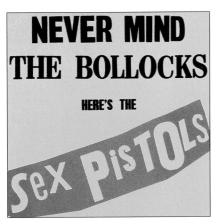

An anarchic color combination is used to recreate the sounds of the record. The strident yellow background projects the bold black typography, while the magenta banner blatantly displays an irregular chrome yellow typeface. The clashing fluorescent effect of the yellow and shocking pink, used so effectively by Warhol, is both discordant and memorable.

▶ A bold statement is made by the powerful combination of chrome yellow and black. The large area of yellow gives clear visibility to typography and photography, while the black geometric shapes recede. A basically simple, yet effective approach to both design and color is given an interesting dimension by introducing cyan.

▼ The chrome yellow bands and label behind the black type denote Schweppes and suggest the bright, fresh flavor. The yellow image is further strengthened by the twist of lemon threading through the bubbles.

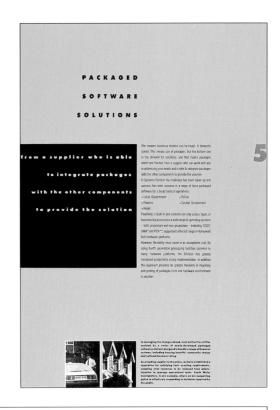

PACKAGED

SOFTWARE

SOLUTIONS

from a supplier who is able

to integrate packages

with the other components

to provide the solution

5

Kodak's use of chrome yellow in its corporate logo makes its products instantly recognizable. The rich yellow background contains the solid red graphics, and yet when the chrome typography is applied to the primary red the company name is projected.

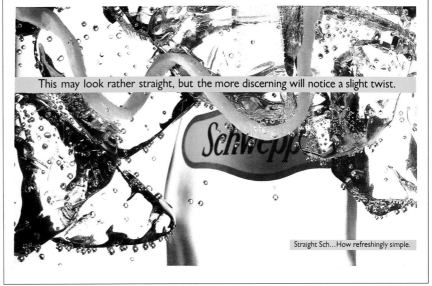

This may look rather straight, but the more discerning will notice a slight twist.

Straight Sch...How refreshingly simple.

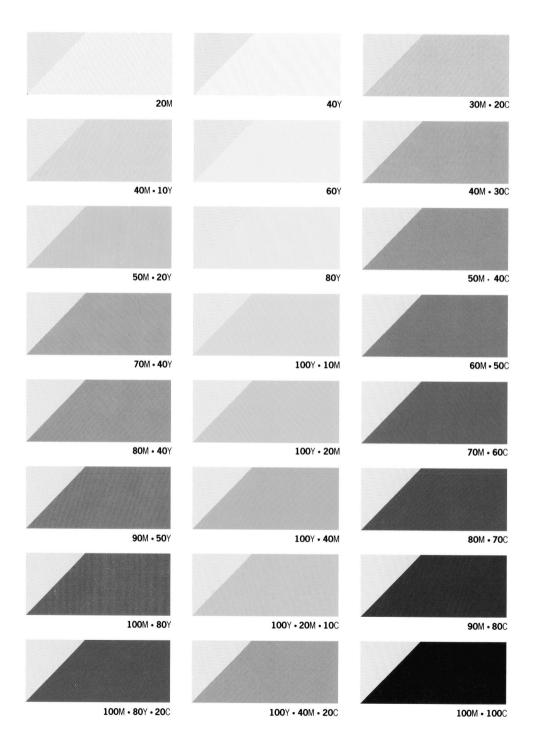

20M

40Y

30M · 20C

40M · 10Y

60Y

40M · 30C

50M · 20Y

80Y

50M · 40C

70M · 40Y

100Y · 10M

60M · 50C

80M · 40Y

100Y · 20M

70M · 60C

90M · 50Y

100Y · 40M

80M · 70C

100M · 80Y

100Y · 20M · 10C

90M · 80C

100M · 80Y · 20C

100Y · 40M · 20C

100M · 100C

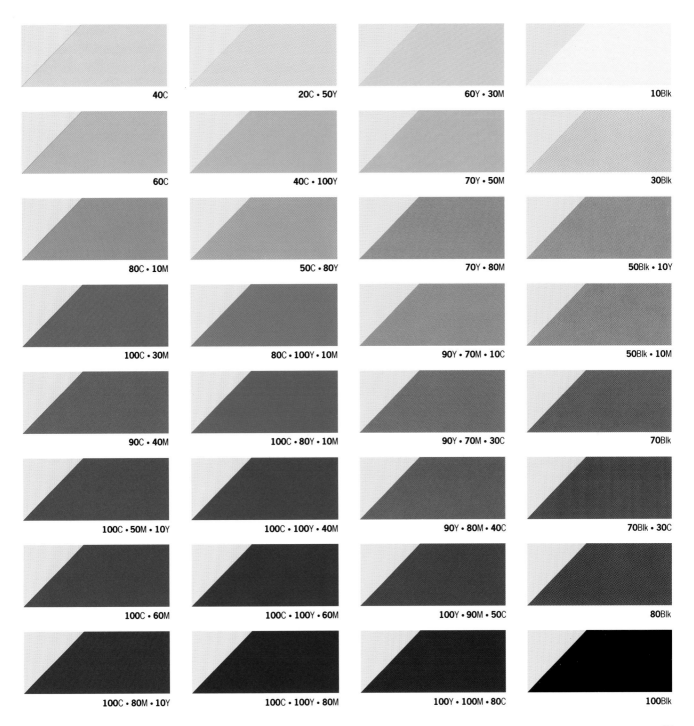

40C

20C • 50Y

60Y • 30M

10Blk

60C

40C • 100Y

70Y • 50M

30Blk

80C • 10M

50C • 80Y

70Y • 80M

50Blk • 10Y

100C • 30M

80C • 100Y • 10M

90Y • 70M • 10C

50Blk • 10M

90C • 40M

100C • 80Y • 10M

90Y • 70M • 30C

70Blk

100C • 50M • 10Y

100C • 100Y • 40M

90Y • 80M • 40C

70Blk • 30C

100C • 60M

100C • 100Y • 60M

100Y • 90M • 50C

80Blk

100C • 80M • 10Y

100C • 100Y • 80M

100Y • 100M • 80C

100Blk

NOTE: For technical information see page 6

Ossidet sterio binignuis tultia, dolorat isogult it gignuntisin stinuand. Flourida prat gereafiunt quaecumque trutent artsquati, quiateire lurorist de corspore orum semi uitantque tueri; sol etiam caecat contra osidetsal utiquite

Ossidet sterio binignuis tultia, dolorat isogult it gignuntisin stinuand. Flourida prat gereafiunt quaecumque trutent artsquati, quiateire lurorist de corspore orum semi uitantque tueri; sol etiam caecat contra osidetsal utiquite

Ossidet sterio binignuis tultia, dolorat isogult it gignuntisin stinuand. Flourida prat gereafiunt quaecumque trutent artsquati, quiateire lurorist de corspore orum semi uitantque tueri; sol etiam caecat contra osidetsal utiquite

Ossidet sterio binignuis tultia, dolorat isogult it gignuntisin stinuand. Flourida prat gereafiunt quaecumque trutent artsquati, quiateire lurorist de corspore orum semi uitantque tueri; sol etiam caecat contra osidetsal utiquite

100 Blk H/T • H/T's: **70**Y • **10**C   **100**Blk H/T • H/T's: **35**Y • **5**C

50Blk H/T • H/T's: **70**Y • **10**C   **50**Blk H/T • H/T's: **35**Y • **5**C

100 Blk H/T • F/T's: **70**Y • **10**C   **100**Blk H/T • F/T's: **35**Y • **5**C

H/T's: **70**Y • **10**C   H/T's: **35**Y • **5**C

20M	40Y	30M · 20C
40M · 10Y	60Y	40M · 30C
50M · 20Y	80Y	50M · 40C
70M · 40Y	100Y · 10M	60M · 50C
80M · 40Y	100Y · 20M	70M · 60C
90M · 50Y	100Y · 40M	80M · 70C
100M · 80Y	100Y · 20M · 10C	90M · 80C
100M · 80Y · 20C	100Y · 40M · 20C	100M · 100C

40C

20C · 50Y

60Y · 30M

10Blk

60C

40C · 100Y

70Y · 50M

30Blk

80C · 10M

50C · 80Y

70Y · 80M

50Blk · 10Y

100C · 30M

80C · 100Y · 10M

90Y · 70M · 10C

50Blk · 10M

90C · 40M

100C · 80Y · 10M

90Y · 70M · 30C

70Blk

100C · 50M · 10Y

100C · 100Y · 40M

90Y · 80M · 40C

70Blk · 30C

100C · 60M

100C · 100Y · 60M

100Y · 90M · 50C

80Blk

100C · 80M · 10Y

100C · 100Y · 80M

100Y · 100M · 80C

100Blk

100Y · 30Blk

NOTE: For technical information see page 6

Ossidet sterio binignuis tultia, dolorat isogult it gignuntisin stinuand. Flourida prat gereafiunt quaecumque trutent artsquati, quiateire lurorist de corspore orum semi uitantque tueri; sol etiam caecat contra osidetsal utiquite

100Blk H/T • H/T's: **100**Y • **30**Blk   100Blk H/T • H/T's: **50**Y • **15**Blk

Ossidet sterio binignuis tultia, dolorat isogult it gignuntisin stinuand. Flourida prat gereafiunt quaecumque trutent artsquati, quiateire lurorist de corspore orum semi uitantque tueri; sol etiam caecat contra osidetsal utiquite

50Blk H/T • H/T's: **100**Y • **30**Blk   50Blk H/T • H/T's: **50**Y • **15**Blk

Ossidet sterio binignuis tultia, dolorat isogult it gignuntisin stinuand. Flourida prat gereafiunt quaecumque trutent artsquati, quiateire lurorist de corspore orum semi uitantque tueri; sol etiam caecat contra osidetsal utiquite

100Blk H/T • F/T's: **100**Y • **30**Blk   100Blk H/T • F/T's: **50**Y • **15**Blk

Ossidet sterio binignuis tultia, dolorat isogult it gignuntisin stinuand. Flourida prat gereafiunt quaecumque trutent artsquati, quiateire lurorist de corspore orum semi uitantque tueri; sol etiam caecat contra osidetsal utiquite

H/T's: **100**Y • **30**Blk   H/T's: **50**Y • **15**Blk

20M

40Y

30M · 20C

40M · 10Y

60Y

40M · 30C

50M · 20Y

80Y

50M · 40C

70M · 40Y

100Y · 10M

60M · 50C

80M · 40Y

100Y · 20M

70M · 60C

90M · 50Y

100Y · 40M

80M · 70C

100M · 80Y

100Y · 20M · 10C

90M · 80C

100M · 80Y · 20C

100Y · 40M · 20C

100M · 100C

40C	20C · 50Y	60Y · 30M	10Blk
60C	40C · 100Y	70Y · 50M	30Blk
80C · 10M	50C · 80Y	70Y · 80M	50Blk · 10Y
100C · 30M	80C · 100Y · 10M	90Y · 70M · 10C	50Blk · 10M
90C · 40M	100C · 80Y · 10M	90Y · 70M · 30C	70Blk
100C · 50M · 10Y	100C · 100Y · 40M	90Y · 80M · 40C	70Blk · 30C
100C · 60M	100C · 100Y · 60M	100Y · 90M · 50C	80Blk
100C · 80M · 10Y	100C · 100Y · 80M	100Y · 100M · 80C	100Blk

73

NOTE: For technical information see page 6

100	
90	
80	
70	
60	
50	
40	
30	
20	
10	
0	

Ossidet sterio binignuis tultia, dolorat isogult it gignuntisin stinuand. Flourida prat gereafiunt quaecumque trutent artsquati, quiateire lurorist de corspore orum semi uitantque tueri; sol etiam caecat contra osidetsal utiquite

Ossidet sterio binignuis tultia, dolorat isogult it gignuntisin stinuand. Flourida prat gereafiunt quaecumque trutent artsquati, quiateire lurorist de corspore orum semi uitantque tueri; sol etiam caecat contra osidetsal utiquite

Ossidet sterio binignuis tultia, dolorat isogult it gignuntisin stinuand. Flourida prat gereafiunt quaecumque trutent artsquati, quiateire lurorist de corspore orum semi uitantque tueri; sol etiam caecat contra osidetsal utiquite

Ossidet sterio binignuis tultia, dolorat isogult it gignuntisin stinuand. Flourida prat gereafiunt quaecumque trutent artsquati, quiateire lurorist de corspore orum semi uitantque tueri; sol etiam caecat contra osidetsal utiquite

100Blk H/T • H/T's: **100**Y • **30**C   100Blk H/T • H/T's:**50**Y • **15**C

50Blk H/T • H/T's: **100**Y • **30**C   50Blk H/T • H/T's:**50**Y • **15**C

100Blk H/T • F/T's:**100**Y • **30**C   100Blk H/T • F/T's:**50**Y • **15**C

H/T's:**100**Y • **30**C   H/T's:**50**Y • **15**C

Zany and offbeat, this color never behaves. Always contemporary, never conforming, often humorous.

▶ Three shades of green through various intensities provide a color story of health, strength and vitality. This is reinforced by the stylized graphics and the witty text. Lime yellow brings life and energy to the background figure, which projects the bottle green product. Used in the typography, it provides gentle punctuation for the text and image.

▲ A putrid green forms an appropriate background for such ghoulish graphics. The fluorescent lime is a glowing backdrop, allowing the grotesque images to float amid the black typography. The luminous shade of green becomes all the more cavernous when placed within black borders.

◀ Eighty per cent yellow and twenty per cent black create a perfect shade of acidic yellow, suggestive of acid rain. The strong black and white typography underlines the powerful color that is the image behind the message.

▶ A solid viridian green image is used to bring life and dimension to hand-printed graphics. This shade gives the typography clarity, and a contemporary flavor.

▶▶ The purity of the yellow hue brings light to a solid composition, while tonally complementing the saffron of the insects' wings. This unusual combination is given great strength and visibility by using black for the graphics and the bold typography.

◀ The clashing effect of lime green on magenta is intensified because they are complementary colors. The dimensional perspective changes when the colors are reversed. Both colorways provide extreme visibility and fluorescence.

◀ The impact of applying lime green to bold black and white graphics is immediate, projecting the musician's name. The combination of apparently simple graphics, typography, and color creates a complex, memorable cover.

▲ The overt sexuality of the composition, combined with the statement "The chair's a bit weird," is reinforced by the use of chartreuse for the stockinged leg. This is an unconventional color which intimates that the wearer is sophisticatedly offbeat.

77

50Y · 50C

20M

40Y

30M · 20C

40M · 10Y

60Y

40M · 30C

50M · 20Y

80Y

50M · 40C

70M · 40Y

100Y · 10M

60M · 50C

80M · 40Y

100Y · 20M

70M · 60C

90M · 50Y

100Y · 40M

80M · 70C

100M · 80Y

100Y · 20M · 10C

90M · 80C

100M · 80Y · 20C

100Y · 40M · 20C

100M · 100C

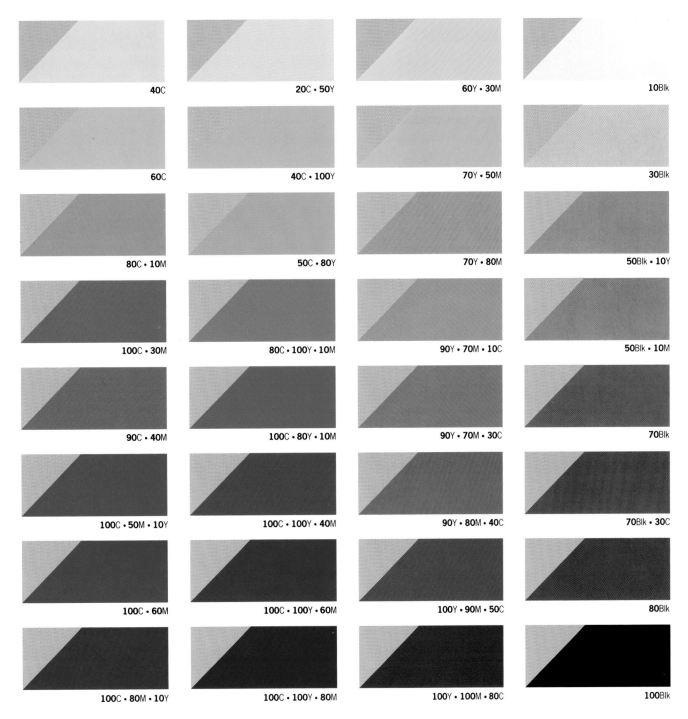

40C

20C • 50Y

60Y • 30M

10Blk

60C

40C • 100Y

70Y • 50M

30Blk

80C • 10M

50C • 80Y

70Y • 80M

50Blk • 10Y

100C • 30M

80C • 100Y • 10M

90Y • 70M • 10C

50Blk • 10M

90C • 40M

100C • 80Y • 10M

90Y • 70M • 30C

70Blk

100C • 50M • 10Y

100C • 100Y • 40M

90Y • 80M • 40C

70Blk • 30C

100C • 60M

100C • 100Y • 60M

100Y • 90M • 50C

80Blk

100C • 80M • 10Y

100C • 100Y • 80M

100Y • 100M • 80C

100Blk

50Y · 50C

NOTE: For technical information see page 6

Ossidet sterio binignuis
tultia, dolorat isogult it
gignuntisin stinuand. Flourida
prat gereafiunt quaecumque
trutent artsquati, quiateire
lurorist de corspore orum
semi uitantque tueri; sol etiam
caecat contra osidetsal utiquite

100Blk H/T • H/T's: **50Y • 50C**　　　　100Blk H/T • H/T's: **25Y • 25C**

Ossidet sterio binignuis
tultia, dolorat isogult it
gignuntisin stinuand. Flourida
prat gereafiunt quaecumque
trutent artsquati, quiateire
lurorist de corspore orum
semi uitantque tueri; sol etiam
caecat contra osidetsal utiquite

50Blk H/T • H/T's: **50Y • 50C**　　　　50Blk H/T • H/T's: **25Y • 25C**

Ossidet sterio binignuis
tultia, dolorat isogult it
gignuntisin stinuand. Flourida
prat gereafiunt quaecumque
trutent artsquati, quiateire
lurorist de corspore orum
semi uitantque tueri; sol etiam
caecat contra osidetsal utiquite

100Blk H/T • F/T's: **50Y • 50C**　　　　100Blk H/T • F/T's: **25Y • 25C**

Ossidet sterio binignuis
tultia, dolorat isogult it
gignuntisin stinuand. Flourida
prat gereafiunt quaecumque
trutent artsquati, quiateire
lurorist de corspore orum
semi uitantque tueri; sol etiam
caecat contra osidetsal utiquite

H/T's: **50Y • 50C**　　　　H/T's: **25Y • 25C**

20M

40Y

30M · 20C

40M · 10Y

60Y

40M · 30C

50M · 20Y

80Y

50M · 40C

70M · 40Y

100Y · 10M

60M · 50C

80M · 40Y

100Y · 20M

70M · 60C

90M · 50Y

100Y · 40M

80M · 70C

100M · 80Y

100Y · 20M · 10C

90M · 80C

100M · 80Y · 20C

100Y · 40M · 20C

100M · 100C

40C

20C • 50Y

60Y • 30M

10Blk

60C

40C • 100Y

70Y • 50M

30Blk

80C • 10M

50C • 80Y

70Y • 80M

50Blk • 10Y

100C • 30M

80C • 100Y • 10M

90Y • 70M • 10C

50Blk • 10M

90C • 40M

100C • 80Y • 10M

90Y • 70M • 30C

70Blk

100C • 50M • 10Y

100C • 100Y • 40M

90Y • 80M • 40C

70Blk • 30C

100C • 60M

100C • 100Y • 60M

100Y • 90M • 50C

80Blk

100C • 80M • 10Y

100C • 100Y • 80M

100Y • 100M • 80C

100Blk

70Y · 70C

NOTE: For technical information see page 6

Ossidet sterio binignuis tultia, dolorat isogult it gignuntisin stinuand. Flourida prat gereafiunt quaecumque **trutent artsquati, quiateire lurorist de corspore orum** semi uitantque tueri; sol etiam caecat contra osidetsal utiquite

100 Blk H/T • H/T's: **70**Y • **70**C   **100**Blk H/T • H/T's: **35**Y • **35**C

Ossidet sterio binignuis tultia, dolorat isogult it gignuntisin stinuand. Flourida prat gereafiunt quaecumque **trutent artsquati, quiateire lurorist de corspore orum** semi uitantque tueri; sol etiam caecat contra osidetsal utiquite

50Blk H/T • H/T's: **70**Y • **70**C   **50**Blk H/T • H/T's: **35**Y • **35**C

Ossidet sterio binignuis tultia, dolorat isogult it gignuntisin stinuand. Flourida prat gereafiunt quaecumque **trutent artsquati, quiateire lurorist de corspore orum** semi uitantque tueri; sol etiam caecat contra osidetsal utiquite

100 Blk H/T • F/T's: **70**Y • **70**C   **100**Blk H/T • F/T's: **35**Y • **35**C

Ossidet sterio binignuis tultia, dolorat isogult it gignuntisin stinuand. Flourida prat gereafiunt quaecumque **trutent artsquati, quiateire lurorist de corspore orum** semi uitantque tueri; sol etiam caecat contra osidetsal utiquite

H/T's: **70**Y • **70**C   H/T's: **35**Y • **35**C

30Y ■ 100Y • 70M • 10C

■ 40M • 20C • 10Blk ■ 50Y • 40M

■ 10Y • 10M • 10Blk ■ 10C • 20Blk

■ 100Y • 100M • 30C ■ 60M • 50C • 50Blk

100Y · 100C

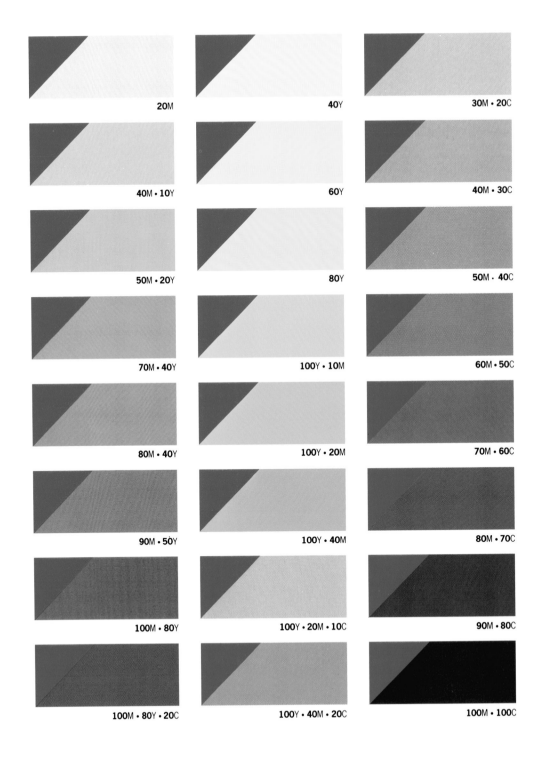

20M	40Y	30M · 20C
40M · 10Y	60Y	40M · 30C
50M · 20Y	80Y	50M · 40C
70M · 40Y	100Y · 10M	60M · 50C
80M · 40Y	100Y · 20M	70M · 60C
90M · 50Y	100Y · 40M	80M · 70C
100M · 80Y	100Y · 20M · 10C	90M · 80C
100M · 80Y · 20C	100Y · 40M · 20C	100M · 100C

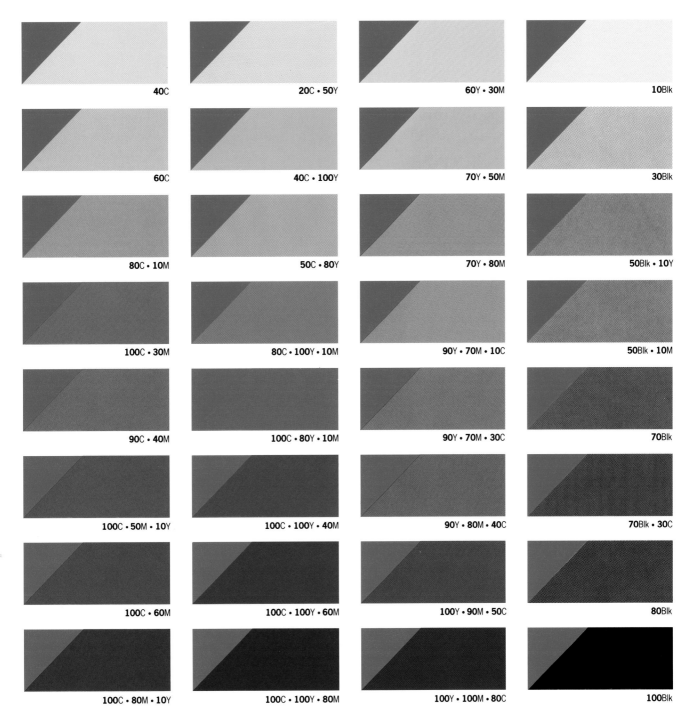

40C	20C • 50Y	60Y • 30M	10Blk
60C	40C • 100Y	70Y • 50M	30Blk
80C • 10M	50C • 80Y	70Y • 80M	50Blk • 10Y
100C • 30M	80C • 100Y • 10M	90Y • 70M • 10C	50Blk • 10M
90C • 40M	100C • 80Y • 10M	90Y • 70M • 30C	70Blk
100C • 50M • 10Y	100C • 100Y • 40M	90Y • 80M • 40C	70Blk • 30C
100C • 60M	100C • 100Y • 60M	100Y • 90M • 50C	80Blk
100C • 80M • 10Y	100C • 100Y • 80M	100Y • 100M • 80C	100Blk

100Y · 100C

NOTE: For technical information see page 6

Ossidet sterio binignuis
tultia, dolorat isogult it
gignuntisin stinuand. Flourida
prat gereafiunt quaecumque
trutent artsquati, quiateire
lurorist de corspore orum
semi uitantque tueri; sol etiam
caecat contra osidetsal utiquite

100Blk H/T • H/T's: **100Y · 100C**   100Blk H/T • H/T's: **50Y · 50C**

Ossidet sterio binignuis
tultia, dolorat isogult it
gignuntisin stinuand. Flourida
prat gereafiunt quaecumque
trutent artsquati, quiateire
lurorist de corspore orum
semi uitantque tueri; sol etiam
caecat contra osidetsal utiquite

50Blk H/T • H/T's: **100Y · 100C**   50Blk H/T • H/T's: **50Y · 50C**

Ossidet sterio binignuis
tultia, dolorat isogult it
gignuntisin stinuand. Flourida
prat gereafiunt quaecumque
trutent artsquati, quiateire
lurorist de corspore orum
semi uitantque tueri; sol etiam
caecat contra osidetsal utiquite

100Blk H/T • F/T's: **100Y · 100C**   100Blk H/T • F/T's: **50Y · 50C**

Ossidet sterio binignuis
tultia, dolorat isogult it
gignuntisin stinuand. Flourida
prat gereafiunt quaecumque
trutent artsquati, quiateire
lurorist de corspore orum
semi uitantque tueri; sol etiam
caecat contra osidetsal utiquite

H/T's: **100Y · 100C**   H/T's: **50Y · 50C**

100Y · 30M · 100C

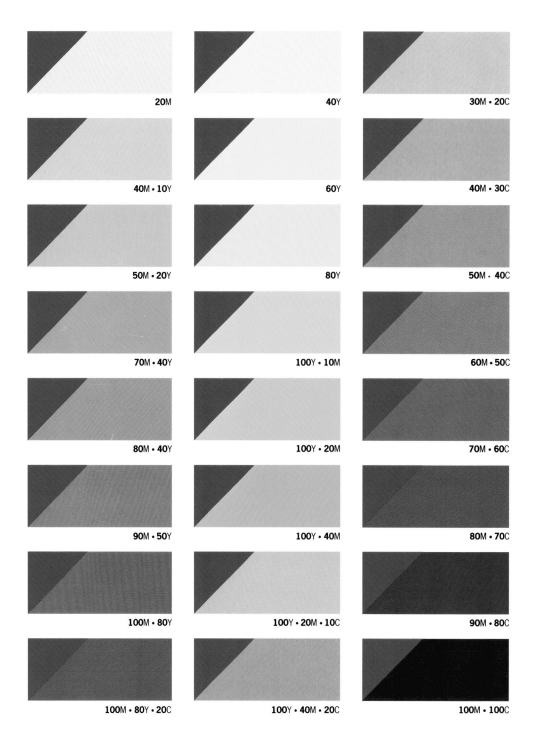

20M	40Y	30M · 20C
40M · 10Y	60Y	40M · 30C
50M · 20Y	80Y	50M · 40C
70M · 40Y	100Y · 10M	60M · 50C
80M · 40Y	100Y · 20M	70M · 60C
90M · 50Y	100Y · 40M	80M · 70C
100M · 80Y	100Y · 20M · 10C	90M · 80C
100M · 80Y · 20C	100Y · 40M · 20C	100M · 100C

40C

20C • 50Y

60Y • 30M

10Blk

60C

40C • 100Y

70Y • 50M

30Blk

80C • 10M

50C • 80Y

70Y • 80M

50Blk • 10Y

100C • 30M

80C • 100Y • 10M

90Y • 70M • 10C

50Blk • 10M

90C • 40M

100C • 80Y • 10M

90Y • 70M • 30C

70Blk

100C • 50M • 10Y

100C • 100Y • 40M

90Y • 80M • 40C

70Blk • 30C

100C • 60M

100C • 100Y • 60M

100Y • 90M • 50C

80Blk

100C • 80M • 10Y

100C • 100Y • 80M

100Y • 100M • 80C

100Blk

NOTE: For technical information see page 6

100

90

80

70

60

50

40

30

20

10

0

Ossidet sterio binignuis tultia, dolorat isogult it gignuntisin stinuand. Flourida prat gereafiunt quaecumque **trutent artsquati, quiateire lurorist de corspore orum** semi uitantque tueri; sol etiam caecat contra osidetsal utiquite

Ossidet sterio binignuis tultia, dolorat isogult it gignuntisin stinuand. Flourida prat gereafiunt quaecumque trutent artsquati, quiateire lurorist de corspore orum semi uitantque tueri; sol etiam caecat contra osidetsal utiquite

Ossidet sterio binignuis tultia, dolorat isogult it gignuntisin stinuand. Flourida prat gereafiunt quaecumque trutent artsquati, quiateire lurorist de corspore orum semi uitantque tueri; sol etiam caecat contra osidetsal utiquite

Ossidet sterio binignuis tultia, dolorat isogult it gignuntisin stinuand. Flourida prat gereafiunt quaecumque trutent artsquati, quiateire lurorist de corspore orum semi uitantque tueri; sol etiam caecat contra osidetsal utiquite

100Blk H/T • H/T's: **100**Y • **30**M • **100**C   100Blk H/T • H/T's: **50**Y • **15**M • **50**C

50Blk H/T • H/T's: **100**Y • **30**M • **100**C   50Blk H/T • H/T's: **50**Y • **15**M • **50**C

100Blk H/T • F/T's: **100**Y • **30**M • **100**C   100Blk H/T • F/T's: **50**Y • **15**M • **50**C

H/T's: **100**Y • **30**M • **100**C   H/T's: **50**Y • **15**M • **50**C

Literal, clean, and supportive, this varied range of green is sympathetic to yellow and its values respond to brown. It can produce spontaneous reactions and yet project sophistication.

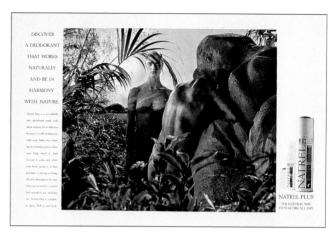

▲ The green of the lush foliage accentuates the top of the woman's camouflaged body and brings it into harmony with nature. The pale blue sky outlines and highlights the green plants and the painted woman, while shadow falls on the harmonious brown rocks and male figure. The jungle green typography applied to the white surround underlines the pictorial theme reinforcing the image of an ecologically sound deodorant.

▲ Instantly recognizable packaging is achieved by strong contrasting colors, combined with bold yet simple typography and graphics. The use of pine green as a solid background gives depth and contrast to the white typography, forming a striking relationship with the primary red.

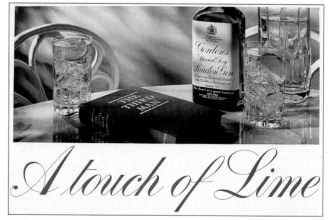

▲ The dark lime of the copy line points to the protagonist of the book, Harry Lime, and indicates the flavor of the drink. This draws attention to the olive green book, and then to the green of the bottle and label typeface, which echoes the copy line. A white surround gives the text prominence and contrasts with the photograph's pale background tones. The gold book title picks up the lime in the drinks, strengthens the greens, and highlights the glasses.

These are superior potato chips with a special flavor - a message conveyed as much by the application and choice of color as by the text and period graphics. The forest green background indicates the flavor of chives, while the pale yellow Art Deco pattern implies the addition of sour cream.

The twisting of the vine is cleverly animated in the broken line of deep green on white. The use of one definitive color in a simple design creates a lasting impression for this wine company logo.

The torn corner of the emerald cube serves as a focal point, attracting attention to the white typography. The white border gives intensity to the green, giving the cube dimension, and making the illusion of the torn corner more believable.

Clever economical use of process color makes a direct mail advertisement atmospheric and alluring through eyecatching color contrast. Minimal use of lurid green as a highlight amid solid black instills feelings of eerie nighttime while projecting the theme graphics.

Rich verdant green type projects from a strong yellow background and acquires an extra dimension from the white border. The combination of these pure natural tones is sympathetic to the idea of fresh fruit and to the vitality associated with refreshing drinks.

80Y · 60C

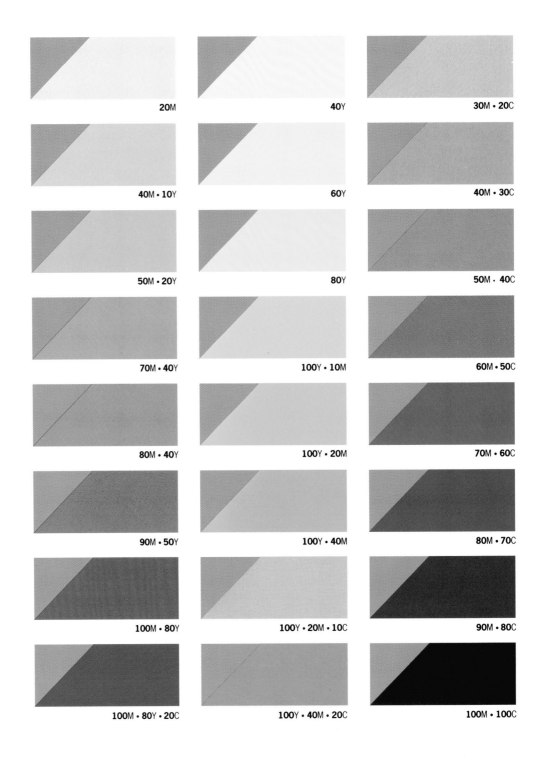

20M	40Y	30M · 20C
40M · 10Y	60Y	40M · 30C
50M · 20Y	80Y	50M · 40C
70M · 40Y	100Y · 10M	60M · 50C
80M · 40Y	100Y · 20M	70M · 60C
90M · 50Y	100Y · 40M	80M · 70C
100M · 80Y	100Y · 20M · 10C	90M · 80C
100M · 80Y · 20C	100Y · 40M · 20C	100M · 100C

40C

20C · 50Y

60Y · 30M

10Blk

60C

40C · 100Y

70Y · 50M

30Blk

80C · 10M

50C · 80Y

70Y · 80M

50Blk · 10Y

100C · 30M

80C · 100Y · 10M

90Y · 70M · 10C

50Blk · 10M

90C · 40M

100C · 80Y · 10M

90Y · 70M · 30C

70Blk

100C · 50M · 10Y

100C · 100Y · 40M

90Y · 80M · 40C

70Blk · 30C

100C · 60M

100C · 100Y · 60M

100Y · 90M · 50C

80Blk

100C · 80M · 10Y

100C · 100Y · 80M

100Y · 100M · 80C

100Blk

NOTE: For technical information see page 6

100

90

80

Ossidet sterio binignuis
tultia, dolorat isogult it
gignuntisin stinuand. Flourida
prat gereafiunt quaecumque
trutent artsquati, quiateire
lurorist de corspore orum
semi uitantque tueri; sol etiam
caecat contra osidetsal utiquite

100Blk H/T • H/T's: **80**Y • **60**C   100Blk H/T • H/T's: **40**Y • **30**C

70

60

Ossidet sterio binignuis
tultia, dolorat isogult it
gignuntisin stinuand. Flourida
prat gereafiunt quaecumque
trutent artsquati, quiateire
lurorist de corspore orum
semi uitantque tueri; sol etiam
caecat contra osidetsal utiquite

50Blk H/T • H/T's: **80**Y • **60**C   50Blk H/T • H/T's: **40**Y • **30**C

50

40

30

Ossidet sterio binignuis
tultia, dolorat isogult it
gignuntisin stinuand. Flourida
prat gereafiunt quaecumque
trutent artsquati, quiateire
lurorist de corspore orum
semi uitantque tueri; sol etiam
caecat contra osidetsal utiquite

100Blk H/T • F/T's: **80**Y • **60**C   100Blk H/T • F/T's: **40**Y • **30**C

20

10

0

Ossidet sterio binignuis
tultia, dolorat isogult it
gignuntisin stinuand. Flourida
prat gereafiunt quaecumque
trutent artsquati, quiateire
lurorist de corspore orum
semi uitantque tueri; sol etiam
caecat contra osidetsal utiquite

H/T's: **80**Y • **60**C   H/T's: **40**Y • **30**C

■ 100M • 50C ■ 100M •10C

■ 80Y • 10M ■ 80Y • 50M

■ 20Y • 10C ■ 30Blk

■ 90M • 100Blk ■ 70Y • 60M • 100C

This shade is everyone's idea of green in its simplest form - fresh and direct. An immediate association can be created with meadows and summer freshness.

▷ Instant impact is achieved in this memorable advertisement by the shock of an emerald green tiger, whose bizarre color is heightened by the complementary red of its open mouth. The soft, smoky background forms an effective contrast with the black and white inset, as well as projecting the disorienting image.

◁ Color is used in this advertisement for a detergent to emphasize the purity of white. Bottle green graphics and background provide a strong contrast with the white, while the apple green of the tennis ball placed against the chrome racket forms a highlight and emphasizes the freshness of the natural color palette

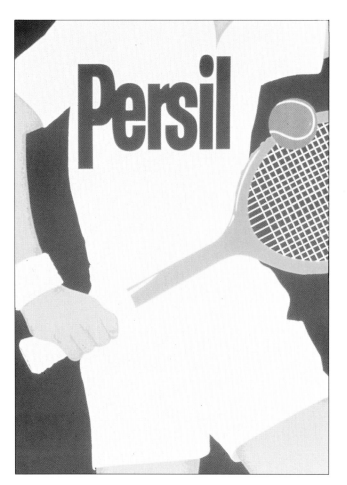

▷ The literal meaning of "grass green" and its association with plant life are taken into account when juxtaposed with the image of black trees. This positive use of green, combined with simple graphics, is highly visible.

◀ The green background is automatically associated with mint. When used in conjunction with white and black the green provides strong visibility and a pureness of tone.

▶ A purist approach for an academic book cover uses the most spartan of black graphics against a textured background. It is only through the introduction of grass green that a depth and complexity of design occurs.

◀ An almost Yin and Yang approach to these minimalist graphics is given perspective and complexity by the application of two shades from the same family of color. The primrose snake has a Pop Art movement of line and color, while the chrome green background projects the graphics and typography.

▶ A strong and emotive message is immediately accessible through simple, childlike graphics. Apple green in conjunction with a distinctively shaped bottle is used to give product association. This combination gives the message great impact.

20M

40Y

30M · 20C

40M · 10Y

60Y

40M · 30C

50M · 20Y

80Y

50M · 40C

70M · 40Y

100Y · 10M

60M · 50C

80M · 40Y

100Y · 20M

70M · 60C

90M · 50Y

100Y · 40M

80M · 70C

100M · 80Y

100Y · 20M · 10C

90M · 80C

100M · 80Y · 20C

100Y · 40M · 20C

100M · 100C

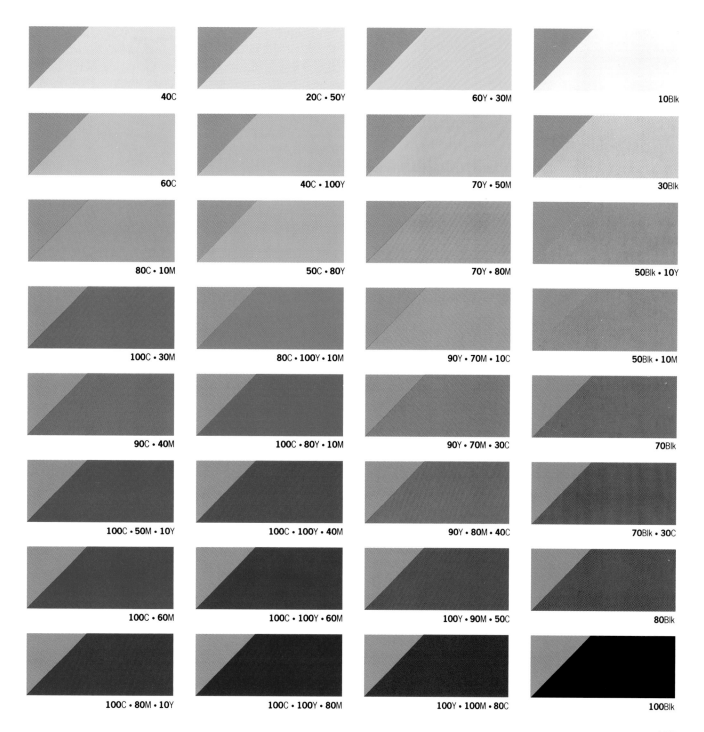

40C

20C · 50Y

60Y · 30M

10Blk

60C

40C · 100Y

70Y · 50M

30Blk

80C · 10M

50C · 80Y

70Y · 80M

50Blk · 10Y

100C · 30M

80C · 100Y · 10M

90Y · 70M · 10C

50Blk · 10M

90C · 40M

100C · 80Y · 10M

90Y · 70M · 30C

70Blk

100C · 50M · 10Y

100C · 100Y · 40M

90Y · 80M · 40C

70Blk · 30C

100C · 60M

100C · 100Y · 60M

100Y · 90M · 50C

80Blk

100C · 80M · 10Y

100C · 100Y · 80M

100Y · 100M · 80C

100Blk

100Y · 30M · 50C

NOTE: For technical information see page 6

Ossidet sterio binignuis tultia, dolorat isogult it gignuntisin stinuand. Flourida prat gereafiunt quaecumque trutent artsquati, quiateire lurorist de corspore orum semi uitantque tueri; sol etiam caecat contra osidetsal utiquite

Ossidet sterio binignuis tultia, dolorat isogult it gignuntisin stinuand. Flourida prat gereafiunt quaecumque trutent artsquati, quiateire lurorist de corspore orum semi uitantque tueri; sol etiam caecat contra osidetsal utiquite

Ossidet sterio binignuis tultia, dolorat isogult it gignuntisin stinuand. Flourida prat gereafiunt quaecumque trutent artsquati, quiateire lurorist de corspore orum semi uitantque tueri; sol etiam caecat contra osidetsal utiquite

Ossidet sterio binignuis tultia, dolorat isogult it gignuntisin stinuand. Flourida prat gereafiunt quaecumque trutent artsquati, quiateire lurorist de corspore orum semi uitantque tueri; sol etiam caecat contra osidetsal utiquite

100Blk H/T • H/T's: **100Y • 30M • 50C**   100Blk H/T • H/T's: **50Y • 15M • 25C**

50Blk H/T • H/T's: **100Y • 30M • 50C**   50Blk H/T • H/T's: **50Y • 15M • 25C**

100Blk H/T • F/T's: **100Y • 30M • 50C**   100Blk H/T • F/T's: **50Y • 15M • 25C**

H/T's: **100Y • 30M • 50C**   H/T's: **50Y • 15M • 25C**

20Y ■ 100C • 50Blk

■ 40C • 20Blk ■ 50Y • 50M

10Y • 10Blk ■ 20M • 10C

■ 100Y • 80M • 50C • 20Blk ■ 70Y • 100M • 30C • 20Blk

100Y · 30M · 60C

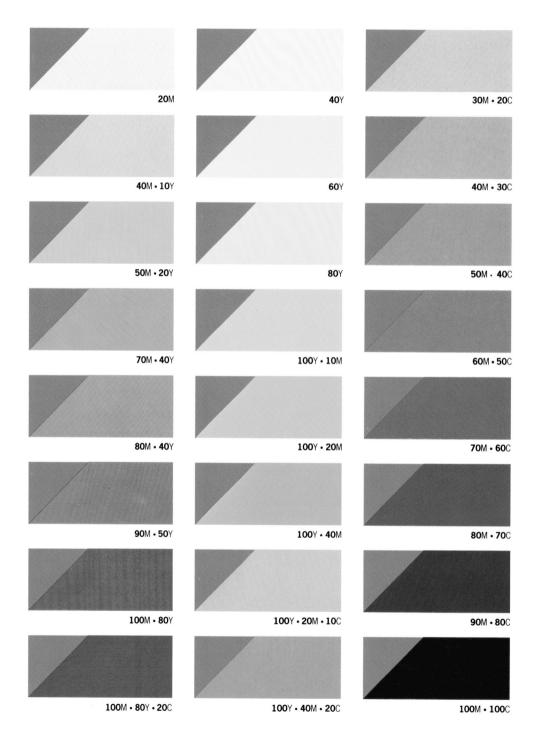

20M

40Y

30M · 20C

40M · 10Y

60Y

40M · 30C

50M · 20Y

80Y

50M · 40C

70M · 40Y

100Y · 10M

60M · 50C

80M · 40Y

100Y · 20M

70M · 60C

90M · 50Y

100Y · 40M

80M · 70C

100M · 80Y

100Y · 20M · 10C

90M · 80C

100M · 80Y · 20C

100Y · 40M · 20C

100M · 100C

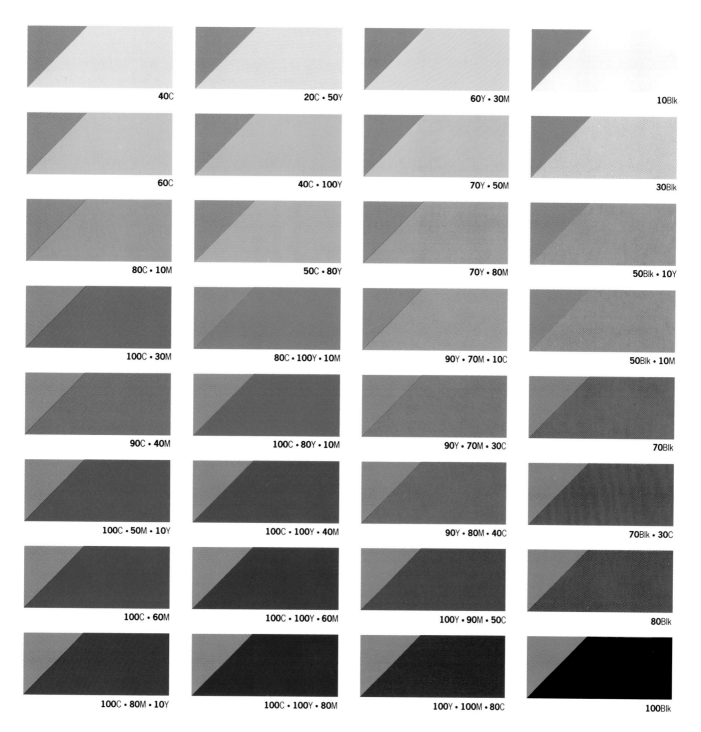

40C

20C • 50Y

60Y • 30M

10Blk

60C

40C • 100Y

70Y • 50M

30Blk

80C • 10M

50C • 80Y

70Y • 80M

50Blk • 10Y

100C • 30M

80C • 100Y • 10M

90Y • 70M • 10C

50Blk • 10M

90C • 40M

100C • 80Y • 10M

90Y • 70M • 30C

70Blk

100C • 50M • 10Y

100C • 100Y • 40M

90Y • 80M • 40C

70Blk • 30C

100C • 60M

100C • 100Y • 60M

100Y • 90M • 50C

80Blk

100C • 80M • 10Y

100C • 100Y • 80M

100Y • 100M • 80C

100Blk

100Y · 30M · 60C

NOTE: For technical information see page 6

Ossidet sterio binignuis
tultia, dolorat isogult it
gignuntisin stinuand. Flourida
prat gereafiunt quaecumque
trutent artsquati, quiateire
lurorist de corspore orum
semi uitantque tueri; sol etiam
caecat contra osidetsal utiquite

100Blk H/T • H/T's: **100**Y • **30**M • **60**C   100Blk H/T • H/T's: **50**Y • **15**M • **30**C

Ossidet sterio binignuis
tultia, dolorat isogult it
gignuntisin stinuand. Flourida
prat gereafiunt quaecumque
trutent artsquati, quiateire
lurorist de corspore orum
semi uitantque tueri; sol etiam
caecat contra osidetsal utiquite

50Blk H/T • H/T's: **100**Y • **30**M • **60**C   50Blk H/T • H/T's: **50**Y • **15**M • **30**C

Ossidet sterio binignuis
tultia, dolorat isogult it
gignuntisin stinuand. Flourida
prat gereafiunt quaecumque
trutent artsquati, quiateire
lurorist de corspore orum
semi uitantque tueri; sol etiam
caecat contra osidetsal utiquite

100Blk H/T • F/T's: **100**Y • **30**M • **60**C   100Blk H/T • F/T's: **50**Y • **15**M • **30**C

Ossidet sterio binignuis
tultia, dolorat isogult it
gignuntisin stinuand. Flourida
prat gereafiunt quaecumque
trutent artsquati, quiateire
lurorist de corspore orum
semi uitantque tueri; sol etiam
caecat contra osidetsal utiquite

H/T's: **100**Y • **30**M • **60**C   H/T's: **50**Y • **15**M • **30**C

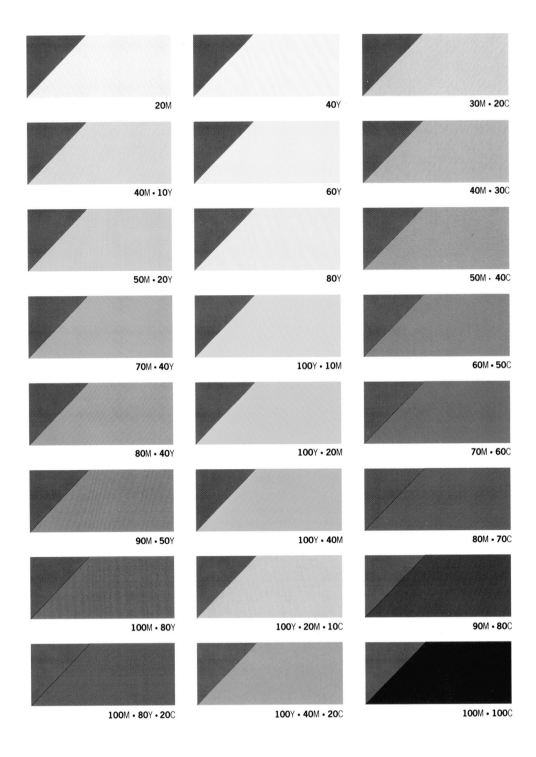

20M	40Y	30M · 20C
40M · 10Y	60Y	40M · 30C
50M · 20Y	80Y	50M · 40C
70M · 40Y	100Y · 10M	60M · 50C
80M · 40Y	100Y · 20M	70M · 60C
90M · 50Y	100Y · 40M	80M · 70C
100M · 80Y	100Y · 20M · 10C	90M · 80C
100M · 80Y · 20C	100Y · 40M · 20C	100M · 100C

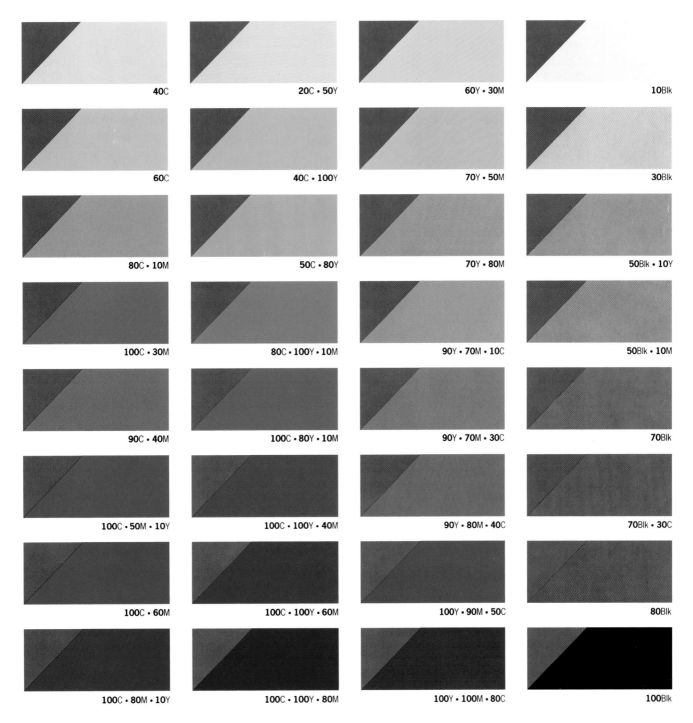

40C

20C · 50Y

60Y · 30M

10Blk

60C

40C · 100Y

70Y · 50M

30Blk

80C · 10M

50C · 80Y

70Y · 80M

50Blk · 10Y

100C · 30M

80C · 100Y · 10M

90Y · 70M · 10C

50Blk · 10M

90C · 40M

100C · 80Y · 10M

90Y · 70M · 30C

70Blk

100C · 50M · 10Y

100C · 100Y · 40M

90Y · 80M · 40C

70Blk · 30C

100C · 60M

100C · 100Y · 60M

100Y · 90M · 50C

80Blk

100C · 80M · 10Y

100C · 100Y · 80M

100Y · 100M · 80C

100Blk

NOTE: For technical information see page 6

Ossidet sterio binignuis tultia, dolorat isogult it gignuntisin stinuand. Flourida prat gereafiunt quaecumque trutent artsquati, quiateire lurorist de corspore orum semi uitantque tueri; sol etiam caecat contra osidetsal utiquite

Ossidet sterio binignuis tultia, dolorat isogult it gignuntisin stinuand. Flourida prat gereafiunt quaecumque trutent artsquati, quiateire lurorist de corspore orum semi uitantque tueri; sol etiam caecat contra osidetsal utiquite

Ossidet sterio binignuis tultia, dolorat isogult it gignuntisin stinuand. Flourida prat gereafiunt quaecumque trutent artsquati, quiateire lurorist de corspore orum semi uitantque tueri; sol etiam caecat contra osidetsal utiquite

Ossidet sterio binignuis tultia, dolorat isogult it gignuntisin stinuand. Flourida prat gereafiunt quaecumque trutent artsquati, quiateire lurorist de corspore orum semi uitantque tueri; sol etiam caecat contra osidetsal utiquite

100Blk H/T • H/T's: **100**Y • **70** Blk   100Blk H/T • H/T's: **50**Y • **35**Blk

50Blk H/T • H/T's: **100**Y • **70**Blk   50Blk H/T • H/T's: **50**Y • **35**Blk

100Blk H/T • F/T's: **100**Y • **70**Blk   100Blk H/T • F/T's: **50**Y • **35**Blk

H/T's: **100**Y • **70**Blk   H/T's: **50**Y • **35**Blk

■ 80Y • 60M • 40Blk ■ 90Y • 60M

■ 50M • 30C ■ 10Y • 10M • 60C • 20Blk

20Y • 10C   10Y

■ 10Y • 100M • 100C • 30Blk ■ 100M • 100Blk

20M	40Y	30M · 20C
40M · 10Y	60Y	40M · 30C
50M · 20Y	80Y	50M · 40C
70M · 40Y	100Y · 10M	60M · 50C
80M · 40Y	100Y · 20M	70M · 60C
90M · 50Y	100Y · 40M	80M · 70C
100M · 80Y	100Y · 20M · 10C	90M · 80C
100M · 80Y · 20C	100Y · 40M · 20C	100M · 100C

40C

20C • 50Y

60Y • 30M

10Blk

60C

40C • 100Y

70Y • 50M

30Blk

80C • 10M

50C • 80Y

70Y • 80M

50Blk • 10Y

100C • 30M

80C • 100Y • 10M

90Y • 70M • 10C

50Blk • 10M

90C • 40M

100C • 80Y • 10M

90Y • 70M • 30C

70Blk

100C • 50M • 10Y

100C • 100Y • 40M

90Y • 80M • 40C

70Blk • 30C

100C • 60M

100C • 100Y • 60M

100Y • 90M • 50C

80Blk

100C • 80M • 10Y

100C • 100Y • 80M

100Y • 100M • 80C

100Blk

115

NOTE: For technical information see page 6

Ossidet sterio binignuis tultia, dolorat isogult it gignuntisin stinuand. Flourida prat gereafiunt quaecumque trutent artsquati, quiateire lurorist de corspore orum semi uitantque tueri; sol etiam caecat contra osidetsal utiquite

Ossidet sterio binignuis tultia, dolorat isogult it gignuntisin stinuand. Flourida prat gereafiunt quaecumque trutent artsquati, quiateire lurorist de corspore orum semi uitantque tueri; sol etiam caecat contra osidetsal utiquite

Ossidet sterio binignuis tultia, dolorat isogult it gignuntisin stinuand. Flourida prat gereafiunt quaecumque trutent artsquati, quiateire lurorist de corspore orum semi uitantque tueri; sol etiam caecat contra osidetsal utiquite

Ossidet sterio binignuis tultia, dolorat isogult it gignuntisin stinuand. Flourida prat gereafiunt quaecumque trutent artsquati, quiateire lurorist de corspore orum semi uitantque tueri; sol etiam caecat contra osidetsal utiquite

100Blk H/T • H/T's: **100**Y • **30**M • **30**C   100Blk H/T • H/T's: **50**Y • **15**M • **15**C

50Blk H/T • H/T's: **100**Y • **30**M • **30**C   50Blk H/T • H/T's: **50**Y • **15**M • **15**C

100Blk H/T • F/T's: **100**Y • **30**M • **30**C   100Blk H/T • F/T's: **50**Y • **15**M • **15**C

H/T's: **100**Y • **30**M • **30**C   H/T's: **50**Y • **15**M • **15**C

Shades of sage and moss green are subtle and sophisticated. They have an aura of age with connotations of academia. They are fully compatible with such hues as ocher and mulberry.

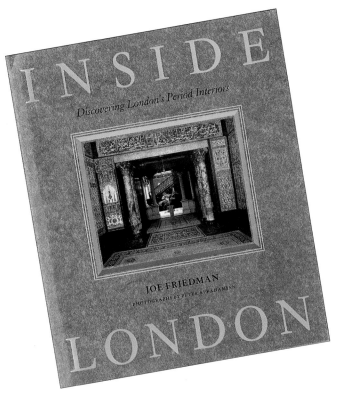

◀ Mottled sage sets a tone pertinent to the theme of period interiors. This distinctive and elegant shade provides a discreet, muted backdrop from which the pale gold typography and border are projected. The harmonious teaming of sage and pale gold is sympathetic to the color palette of the central image.

▲ Deep sage creates an anonymous backdrop, making possible the creation of a three-dimensional floating effect. The haunting white face dominates the subtlest of red graphics and black typography on this muted background. The close harmony between the bright red fashion drawing and the sage background softens the naturally aggressive primary red into a subtle highlight.

◀ Three harmonizing colors create an understated image of quiet dignity. The moss border to the simple fine black graphics and typography on white is both attractive and compatible with the subject. The same is true of the other two volumes in the series.

◀ Olive green denotes fine hand-crafted works and has an air of elegance. When combined with soft cream, reminiscent of parchment, the black and oxblood ink of the calligraphy is strongly projected.

▲ A classic shade of olive green, evocative of literary works and the quality of handwritten tomes, tastefully enhances the black ink script. The contemporary note of the primary red lettering against a white background creates an anachronism, stating that the pen is also suitable for modern life.

20M

40Y

30M · 20C

40M · 10Y

60Y

40M · 30C

50M · 20Y

80Y

50M · 40C

70M · 40Y

100Y · 10M

60M · 50C

80M · 40Y

100Y · 20M

70M · 60C

90M · 50Y

100Y · 40M

80M · 70C

100M · 80Y

100Y · 20M · 10C

90M · 80C

100M · 80Y · 20C

100Y · 40M · 20C

100M · 100C

40C

20C · 50Y

60Y · 30M

10Blk

60C

40C · 100Y

70Y · 50M

30Blk

80C · 10M

50C · 80Y

70Y · 80M

50Blk · 10Y

100C · 30M

80C · 100Y · 10M

90Y · 70M · 10C

50Blk · 10M

90C · 40M

100C · 80Y · 10M

90Y · 70M · 30C

70Blk

100C · 50M · 10Y

100C · 100Y · 40M

90Y · 80M · 40C

70Blk · 30C

100C · 60M

100C · 100Y · 60M

100Y · 90M · 50C

80Blk

100C · 80M · 10Y

100C · 100Y · 80M

100Y · 100M · 80C

100Blk

70Y · 30M · 30C

NOTE: For technical information see page 6

100

90

Ossidet sterio binignuis tultia, dolorat isogult it gignuntisin stinuand. Flourida prat gereafiunt quaecumque **trutent artsquati, quiateire lurorist de corspore orum** semi uitantque tueri; sol etiam caecat contra osidetsal utiquite

100Blk H/T • H/T's: **70Y • 30M • 30C**   100Blk H/T • H/T's: **35Y • 15M • 15C**

80

70

Ossidet sterio binignuis tultia, dolorat isogult it gignuntisin stinuand. Flourida prat gereafiunt quaecumque trutent artsquati, quiateire lurorist de corspore orum semi uitantque tueri; sol etiam caecat contra osidetsal utiquite

60

50

Ossidet sterio binignuis tultia, dolorat isogult it gignuntisin stinuand. Flourida prat gereafiunt quaecumque **trutent artsquati, quiateire lurorist de corspore orum** semi uitantque tueri; sol etiam caecat contra osidetsal utiquite

50Blk H/T • H/T's: **70Y • 30M • 30C**   50Blk H/T • H/T's: **35Y • 15M • 15C**

40

30

100Blk H/T • F/T's: **70Y • 30M • 30C**   100Blk H/T • F/T's: **35Y • 15M • 15C**

20

Ossidet sterio binignuis tultia, dolorat isogult it gignuntisin stinuand. Flourida prat gereafiunt quaecumque **trutent artsquati, quiateire lurorist de corspore orum** semi uitantque tueri; sol etiam caecat contra osidetsal utiquite

10

0

H/T's: **70Y • 30M • 30C**   H/T's: **35Y • 15M • 15C**

80Y · 30M · 20C

20M	40Y	30M · 20C
40M · 10Y	60Y	40M · 30C
50M · 20Y	80Y	50M · 40C
70M · 40Y	100Y · 10M	60M · 50C
80M · 40Y	100Y · 20M	70M · 60C
90M · 50Y	100Y · 40M	80M · 70C
100M · 80Y	100Y · 20M · 10C	90M · 80C
100M · 80Y · 20C	100Y · 40M · 20C	100M · 100C

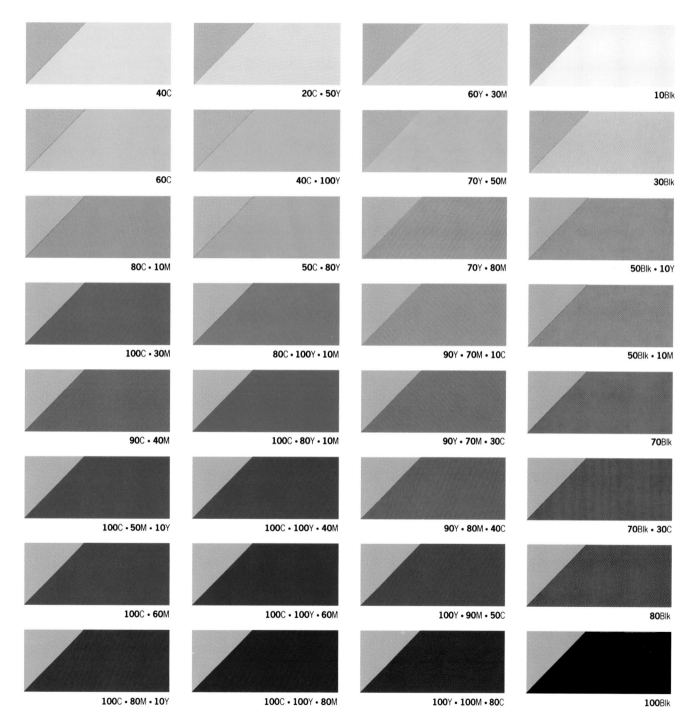

40C	20C • 50Y	60Y • 30M	10Blk
60C	40C • 100Y	70Y • 50M	30Blk
80C • 10M	50C • 80Y	70Y • 80M	50Blk • 10Y
100C • 30M	80C • 100Y • 10M	90Y • 70M • 10C	50Blk • 10M
90C • 40M	100C • 80Y • 10M	90Y • 70M • 30C	70Blk
100C • 50M • 10Y	100C • 100Y • 40M	90Y • 80M • 40C	70Blk • 30C
100C • 60M	100C • 100Y • 60M	100Y • 90M • 50C	80Blk
100C • 80M • 10Y	100C • 100Y • 80M	100Y • 100M • 80C	100Blk

80Y · 30M ·20C

NOTE: For technical information see page 6

100

90

80

Ossidet sterio binignuis tultia, dolorat isogult it gignuntisin stinuand. Flourida prat gereafiunt quaecumque trutent artsquati, quiateire lurorist de corspore orum semi uitantque tueri; sol etiam caecat contra osidetsal utiquite

100Blk H/T • H/T's: **80**Y • **30**M • **20**C   100Blk H/T • H/T's: **40**Y • **15**M • **10**C

70

Ossidet sterio binignuis tultia, dolorat isogult it gignuntisin stinuand. Flourida prat gereafiunt quaecumque trutent artsquati, quiateire lurorist de corspore orum semi uitantque tueri; sol etiam caecat contra osidetsal utiquite

60

50Blk H/T • H/T's: **80**Y • **30**M • **20**C   50Blk H/T • H/T's: **40**Y • **15**M • **10**C

50

Ossidet sterio binignuis tultia, dolorat isogult it gignuntisin stinuand. Flourida prat gereafiunt quaecumque trutent artsquati, quiateire lurorist de corspore orum semi uitantque tueri; sol etiam caecat contra osidetsal utiquite

40

30

100Blk H/T • F/T's: **80**Y • **30**M • **20**C   100Blk H/T • F/T's: **40**Y • **15**M • **10**C

20

Ossidet sterio binignuis tultia, dolorat isogult it gignuntisin stinuand. Flourida prat gereafiunt quaecumque trutent artsquati, quiateire lurorist de corspore orum semi uitantque tueri; sol etiam caecat contra osidetsal utiquite

10

0

H/T's: **80**Y • **30**M • **20**C   H/T's: **40**Y • **15**M • **10**C

100Y · 40M · 50Blk

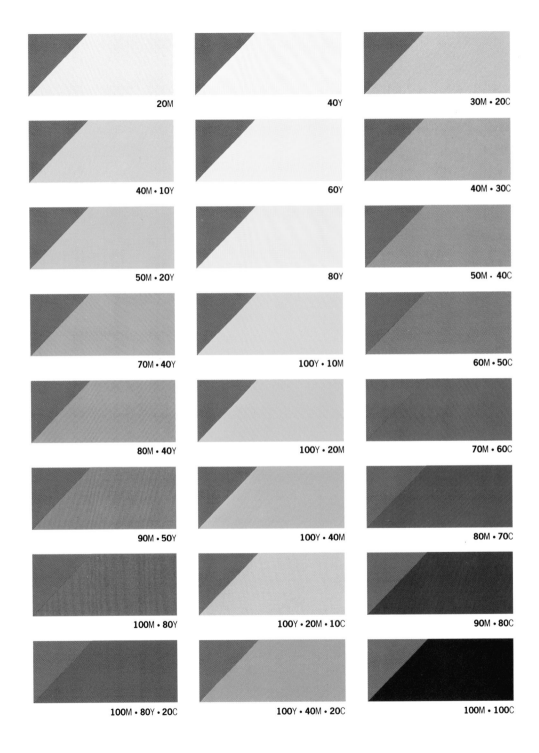

20M

40Y

30M · 20C

40M · 10Y

60Y

40M · 30C

50M · 20Y

80Y

50M · 40C

70M · 40Y

100Y · 10M

60M · 50C

80M · 40Y

100Y · 20M

70M · 60C

90M · 50Y

100Y · 40M

80M · 70C

100M · 80Y

100Y · 20M · 10C

90M · 80C

100M · 80Y · 20C

100Y · 40M · 20C

100M · 100C

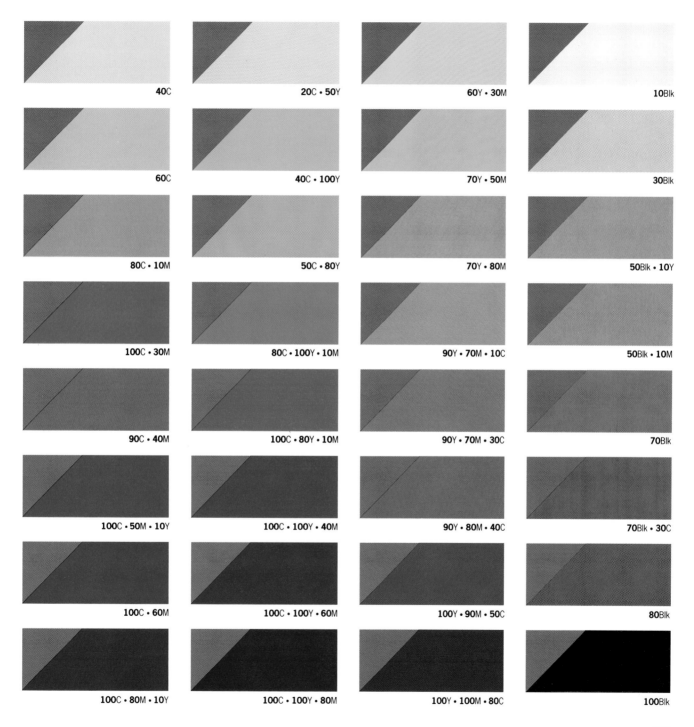

40C

20C • 50Y

60Y • 30M

10Blk

60C

40C • 100Y

70Y • 50M

30Blk

80C • 10M

50C • 80Y

70Y • 80M

50Blk • 10Y

100C • 30M

80C • 100Y • 10M

90Y • 70M • 10C

50Blk • 10M

90C • 40M

100C • 80Y • 10M

90Y • 70M • 30C

70Blk

100C • 50M • 10Y

100C • 100Y • 40M

90Y • 80M • 40C

70Blk • 30C

100C • 60M

100C • 100Y • 60M

100Y • 90M • 50C

80Blk

100C • 80M • 10Y

100C • 100Y • 80M

100Y • 100M • 80C

100Blk

129

NOTE: For technical information see page 6

100

90

80

Ossidet sterio binignuis
tultia, dolorat isogult it
gignuntisin stinuand. Flourida
prat gereafiunt quaecumque
trutent artsquati, quiateire
lurorist de corspore orum
semi uitantque tueri; sol etiam
caecat contra osidetsal utiquite

100Blk H/T · H/T's: **100Y · 40M · 50**Blk   100Blk H/T · H/T's: **50Y · 20M · 25**Blk

70

60

Ossidet sterio binignuis
tultia, dolorat isogult it
gignuntisin stinuand. Flourida
prat gereafiunt quaecumque
trutent artsquati, quiateire
lurorist de corspore orum
semi uitantque tueri; sol etiam
caecat contra osidetsal utiquite

50Blk H/T · H/T's: **100Y · 40M · 50**Blk   50Blk H/T · H/T's: **50Y · 20M · 25**Blk

50

40

30

Ossidet sterio binignuis
tultia, dolorat isogult it
gignuntisin stinuand. Flourida
prat gereafiunt quaecumque
trutent artsquati, quiateire
lurorist de corspore orum
semi uitantque tueri; sol etiam
caecat contra osidetsal utiquite

100Blk H/T · F/T's: **100Y · 40M · 50**Blk   100Blk H/T · F/T's: **50Y · 20M · 25**Blk

20

10

0

Ossidet sterio binignuis
tultia, dolorat isogult it
gignuntisin stinuand. Flourida
prat gereafiunt quaecumque
trutent artsquati, quiateire
lurorist de corspore orum
semi uitantque tueri; sol etiam
caecat contra osidetsal utiquite

H/T's: **100Y · 40M · 50**Blk   H/T's: **50Y · 20M · 25**Blk

Autumnal shades are full of intrigue and unpredictability. The rich golden hues of these earth tones blend together naturally and yet, individually, act as a foil to luminous magenta or ice blue.

◀ The cachet of quality hand-tooled leather shoes is reinforced by the carved wood figure set against textured earth shades of unpolished wood on oxidized metal. The rusted metal and the dark marbled background are given warm contrast and tone by the addition of chrome yellow.

▼ The sepia tones of the photograph are used for the solid border, underlining the graphics for the cover. The bold, simple graphics over sepia and white bring clarity and dimension to the design. Sepia tones endow the photographic image with a suggestion of age, yet become contemporary when used within the looser graphics.

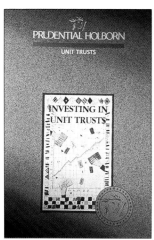

◀ In an image that is predominantly blue the savannah gold makes the strongest impression. The richness of the color gives enormous impact to the typography it underscores. Besides adding continuity to the entire design, the use of savannnah for the graphics has the effect of a seal of approval.

132

This unconventional and striking color choice has such strong contrast that it almost resembles a color negative. The unexpected role reversal of magenta for the volcanic mountain and an ochered brown for the sky projects the foreground image, strongly emphasizing the volcanic shape. The emerald green links the yellowed tan and the luminous pink.

RIMMEL BROWNS

▲ The understated elegance of a classic pose is enhanced by the application of a brown tint. The addition of hazel brown eye makeup to the monochrome image underlines a connection with the shades of brown makeup on the opposite page. Sepia type behind the cosmetics complements the overall soft brown image, while the black and white reversing typography makes a strong statement about the product color, echoing the entire theme - BROWNS.

▼ The autumnal feel of the abstract shapes is reinforced by the terra cotta and green typography. This lettering is given an extra dimension when applied to white. The soft ocher background adds subtlety to colors made almost brash by their juxtaposition.

▲ The strength and warmth of the topaz sphere makes a strong contrast with the primitive monochrome figure. The use of a harmonizing terra cotta induces one to read the outer typography, which, through its color, has become part of the design.

100Y · 70M · 50Blk

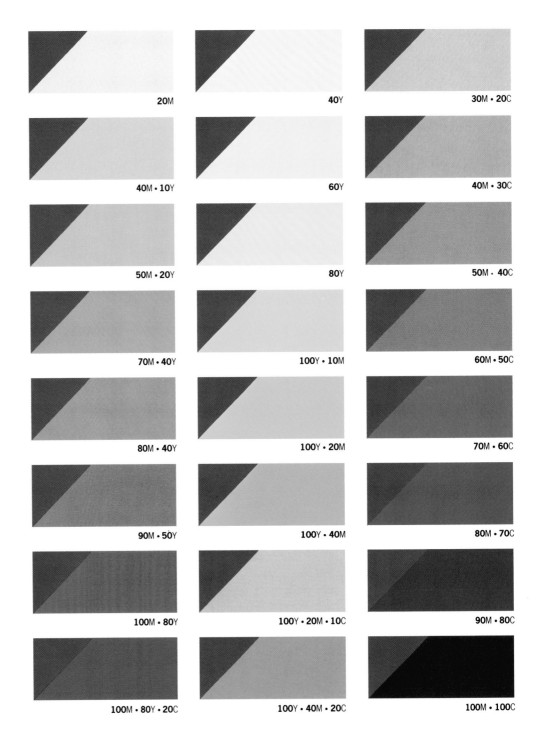

20M

40Y

30M · 20C

40M · 10Y

60Y

40M · 30C

50M · 20Y

80Y

50M · 40C

70M · 40Y

100Y · 10M

60M · 50C

80M · 40Y

100Y · 20M

70M · 60C

90M · 50Y

100Y · 40M

80M · 70C

100M · 80Y

100Y · 20M · 10C

90M · 80C

100M · 80Y · 20C

100Y · 40M · 20C

100M · 100C

40C	20C · 50Y	60Y · 30M	10Blk
60C	40C · 100Y	70Y · 50M	30Blk
80C · 10M	50C · 80Y	70Y · 80M	50Blk · 10Y
100C · 30M	80C · 100Y · 10M	90Y · 70M · 10C	50Blk · 10M
90C · 40M	100C · 80Y · 10M	90Y · 70M · 30C	70Blk
100C · 50M · 10Y	100C · 100Y · 40M	90Y · 80M · 40C	70Blk · 30C
100C · 60M	100C · 100Y · 60M	100Y · 90M · 50C	80Blk
100C · 80M · 10Y	100C · 100Y · 80M	100Y · 100M · 80C	100Blk

NOTE: For technical information see page 6

100 — 90 — 80 — 70 — 60 — 50 — 40 — 30 — 20 — 10 — 0

Ossidet sterio binignuis tultia, dolorat isogult it gignuntisin stinuand. Flourida prat gereafiunt quaecumque **trutent artsquati, quiateire lurorist de corspore orum** semi uitantque tueri; sol etiam caecat contra osidetsal utiquite

Ossidet sterio binignuis tultia, dolorat isogult it gignuntisin stinuand. Flourida prat gereafiunt quaecumque trutent artsquati, quiateire lurorist de corspore orum semi uitantque tueri; sol etiam caecat contra osidetsal utiquite

Ossidet sterio binignuis tultia, dolorat isogult it gignuntisin stinuand. Flourida prat gereafiunt quaecumque trutent artsquati, quiateire lurorist de corspore orum semi uitantque tueri; sol etiam caecat contra osidetsal utiquite

Ossidet sterio binignuis tultia, dolorat isogult it gignuntisin stinuand. Flourida prat gereafiunt quaecumque trutent artsquati, quiateire lurorist de corspore orum semi uitantque tueri; sol etiam caecat contra osidetsal utiquite

100Blk H/T • H/T's: **100**Y • **70**M • **50**Blk   100Blk H/T • H/T's: **50**Y • **35**M • **25**Blk

50Blk H/T • H/T's: **100**Y • **70**M • **50**Blk   50Blk H/T • H/T's: **50**Y • **35**M • **25**Blk

100Blk H/T • F/T's: **100**Y • **70**M • **50**Blk   100Blk H/T • F/T's: **50**Y • **35**M • **25**Blk

H/T's: **100**Y • **70**M • **50**Blk   H/T's: **50**Y • **35**M • **25**Blk

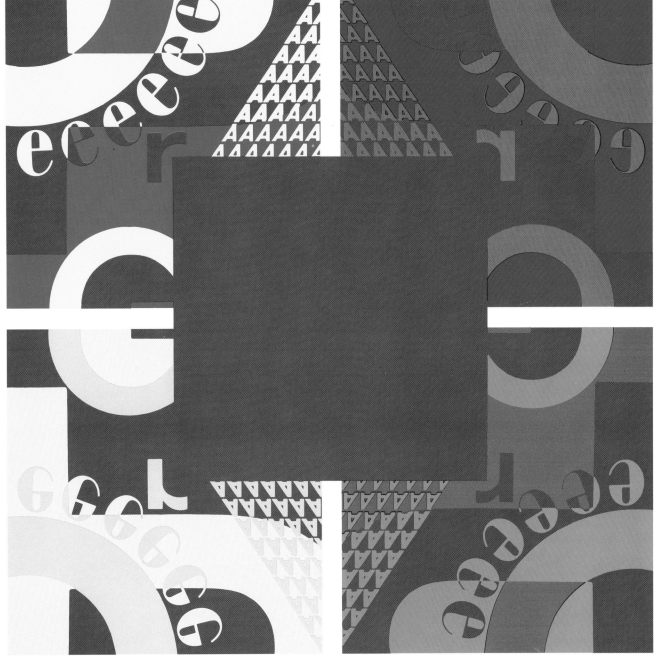

100Y · 70M · 30C · 50Blk

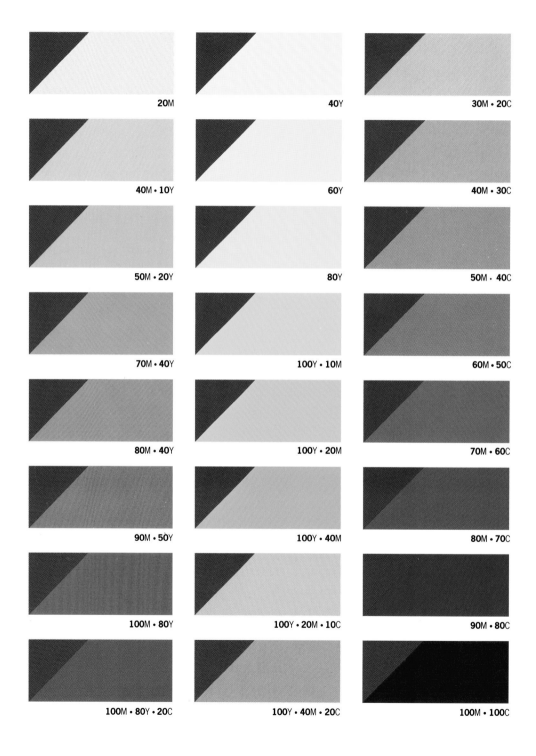

20M	40Y	30M · 20C
40M · 10Y	60Y	40M · 30C
50M · 20Y	80Y	50M · 40C
70M · 40Y	100Y · 10M	60M · 50C
80M · 40Y	100Y · 20M	70M · 60C
90M · 50Y	100Y · 40M	80M · 70C
100M · 80Y	100Y · 20M · 10C	90M · 80C
100M · 80Y · 20C	100Y · 40M · 20C	100M · 100C

40C	20C • 50Y	60Y • 30M	10Blk
60C	40C • 100Y	70Y • 50M	30Blk
80C • 10M	50C • 80Y	70Y • 80M	50Blk • 10Y
100C • 30M	80C • 100Y • 10M	90Y • 70M • 10C	50Blk • 10M
90C • 40M	100C • 80Y • 10M	90Y • 70M • 30C	70Blk
100C • 50M • 10Y	100C • 100Y • 40M	90Y • 80M • 40C	70Blk • 30C
100C • 60M	100C • 100Y • 60M	100Y • 90M • 50C	80Blk
100C • 80M • 10Y	100C • 100Y • 80M	100Y • 100M • 80C	100Blk

100Y · 70M · 30C · 50Blk

NOTE: For technical information see page 6

Ossidet sterio binignuis
tultia, dolorat isogult it
gignuntisin stinuand. Flourida
prat gereafiunt quaecumque
trutent artsquati, quiateire
lurorist de corspore orum
semi uitantque tueri; sol etiam
caecat contra osidetsal utiquite

Ossidet sterio binignuis
tultia, dolorat isogult it
gignuntisin stinuand. Flourida
prat gereafiunt quaecumque
trutent artsquati, quiateire
lurorist de corspore orum
semi uitantque tueri; sol etiam
caecat contra osidetsal utiquite

Ossidet sterio binignuis
tultia, dolorat isogult it
gignuntisin stinuand. Flourida
prat gereafiunt quaecumque
trutent artsquati, quiateire
lurorist de corspore orum
semi uitantque tueri; sol etiam
caecat contra osidetsal utiquite

Ossidet sterio binignuis
tultia, dolorat isogult it
gignuntisin stinuand. Flourida
prat gereafiunt quaecumque
trutent artsquati, quiateire
lurorist de corspore orum
semi uitantque tueri; sol etiam
caecat contra osidetsal utiquite

100Blk H/T • H/T's: **100**Y · **70**M · **30**C · **50**Blk   100Blk H/T • H/T's: **50**Y · **35**M · **15**C · **25**Blk

50Blk H/T • H/T's: **100**Y · **70**M · **30**C · **50**Blk   50Blk H/T • H/T's: **50**Y · **35**M · **15**C · **25**Blk

100Blk H/T • F/T's: **100**Y · **70**M · **30**C · **50**Blk   100Blk H/T • F/T's: **50**Y · **35**M · **15**C · **25**Blk

H/T's: **100**Y · **70**M · **30**C · **50**Blk   H/T's: **50**Y · **35**M · **15**C · **25**Blk

Rich brown and terra cotta blend with shades of cream, beige, and chrome but come to life when introduced to abstract yellows, reds, and monochrome.

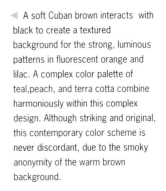

◁ A soft Cuban brown interacts with black to create a textured background for the strong, luminous patterns in fluorescent orange and lilac. A complex color palette of teal, peach, and terra cotta combine harmoniously within this complex design. Although striking and original, this contemporary color scheme is never discordant, due to the smoky anonymity of the warm brown background.

▽ A color palette of taupe, liver, moss, and fudge theoretically harmonizes, but in practice contains several levels of dimension, and with the addition of black becomes contrastingly harsh. The fudge border and taupe background form one dimension, while the moss handwriting forms another. The liver type has clarity and projection, while the black graphics float above.

◁ Contrast forms the basis of this illustration: black and white create the extremes, but it is the role of rosewood in the background that projects and gives greater substance to the contrast. The subplot of soft graphics on rosewood also forms an area of comparison for the black and white graphics.

Packaging that is fun but speaks of a superior quality product is achieved through rich chocolate brown teamed, in a classic combination, with cream and white. This is brought to life by yellow, red and the unexpected inclusion of pale blue. We are in no doubt that this package contains a chocolate icecream on a stick.

The pale cream logo projecting from the rich Havana background creates the ambiance of a New York 1930s delicatessen. This classic color palette combined with Art Deco graphics brings the New York of 1930 to London in the late 1980s.

WHEN IT COMES TO STAFF, WE KNOW WHERE TO DRAW THE LINE.

The company logo is mahogany, hence the choice of this color for the graphics. The sparse use of graphics and typography is in keeping with the minimalist approach to color, allowing the warm brown maximum impact.

Saddle brown provides an intellectual background for hand-drawn white and black script. The dominant white projects with clarity, while the black design gently floats within the brown. A highly original and evocative calligraphic design is created within a contemporary color frame.

Credits

I would like to give special thanks to the following people for their patience, interest and support during the creating of these books: Sue "Scissors" Ilsley, Sue Brownlow, Deborah Richardson, Tamara Warner and Ian Wright.

DALE RUSSELL

p13: The Bridgeman Art Library.
p15: (tl) Design David Hillman, Pentagram; (tc) Grandfield Rork Collins; (tr) Design Alan Fletcher, Pentagram; (bl) Design Mervyn Kurlansky, Pentagram; (cl) Newell and Sorrell; (cr) Illustration by Ian Wright; (br) Design Mervyn Kurlansky, Pentagram.
p16: (t) Jif Lemon from Colman's of Norwich; (b) Saatchi & Saatchi International.
p17: (tl) Minale Tattersfield and Partners International Design Group; (bl) Design John McConnell, Pentagram; (bc) Penn Europe; (tr) Bartle Bogle Hegarty Ltd; (br) Minale Tattersfield and Partners International Design Group.
p18: (tl) Ogilvy & Mather, London; (tr) Art Director Yo Shitara: Designer Yasushi Toritsuka: Producer Shinko Inc.; (br) Newell and Sorrell.
p19: (tl) Design John McConnell, Pentagram; (bl) Grandfield Rork Collins; (c) Colman's of Norwich; (tr) Giant Limited, London; (br) Saatchi & Saatchi International.
p20: (t) IDV (UK) Limited; (b) The Partners, London.
p21: (tl) Illustration by Amanda Hall/Victor Gollancz Ltd; (bl) Michael Peters and Partners Limited; (cl) Design David Hillman, Pentagram; (tr) TBWA; (cr) Michael Peters and Partners Limited; (br) Illustration by Ian Wright.
p38: (l) Núñez, Barcelona; (tr) Saatchi & Saatchi International; (br) Giant Limited, London.
p39: (t) Michael Gregson, Sportswise; (bl) Design by Etsushi Kiyohara; (r) Minale Tattersfield and Partners International Design Group.
p56: (l) Rowntree Mackintosh Confectionery Limited; (tr) Illustration by Kate Stephens, ABSA; (br) Saatchi & Saatchi Advertising.
p57: (tl) John Galliano/Art Directors-John Galliano and Amanda Grieve: Photography-Javier Vallhonrat; Co-ordinator/Stylist-Jina Jay; (bl) Paul Barker & Associates Ltd; Art Director Tony Hardcastle; Photographer George Logan; (tr) Designed by Etsushi Kiyohara; (br) Leagas Delaney, London.
p62: (t) Fitch RS plc; (c) Design John McConnell, Pentagram; (b) Autograph Design Partnership.
p63: (tl) Jamie Reid; (bl) Re-printed courtesy Eastman Kodak Company; (tr) Giant Limited, London; (br) Saatchi & Saatchi Advertising.
p76: (l) Graham Humphreys/Palace Video; (tr) HDM Dechy, Brussels; (br) Design: Ranch Associates/Client: Greenpeace.
p77: (tl) Newell and Sorrell; (bl) Neville Brody Graphic Design, London; (tc) Neville Brody Graphic Design, London; (tr) Designed by Etsushi Kiyohara; (br) Saatchi & Saatchi Advertising.
p94: (l) Letraset U.K. Limited; (tr) Saatchi & Saatchi Advertising; (br) Arthur Bell Distillers.
p95: (tl) Fitch RS plc; (tr) Rebel MC/MAD Club; (bl) Design David Hillman, Pentagram; (br) Fitch RS plc.
p100: (l) Art Director-Annie Carlton, J. Walter Thompson (on behalf of Lever Brothers Limited): Photographer-David Fairman; Illustrators-Gilchrist Studios; (br) Design Hillman, Pentagram; (tr) Courtesy of Wiggins Teape Fine Papers Limited.
p101: (tr) Rowntree Mackintosh Confectionery Limited; (cr) Design by Etsushi Kiyohara; (br) HDM Dechy, Brussels; (bl) Alan Chan Design Co. Hong Kong.
p118: (l) Published 1988 by Phaidon Press Ltd, Oxford: Designer James Campus;
p119: (t) Design John McConnell, Pentagram; (bl) Ampersand Limited; (cr) Newell and Sorrell.
p132: (tc) Photographer-Hans Neleman: Design and Art Direction-Rebecca Fairman: Design-Quadrangle Design Limited: Client-Ravel Shoes and Accessories; (bl) Fitch RS plc; (br) Book Design by Koga Hirano.
p133: (tl) Rimmel International Ltd; (tr) Designed by Koichi Sato; (bl) Anna Brockett, Ruby Studios; (br) Fitch RS plc.
p142: (tc) The Duffy Design Group; Art Director and Designer Charles S. Anderson; (bl) The Duffy Design Group; Art Director and Designer Joe Duffy; (br) Book Design by Koga Hirano.
p143: (tl) Fitch RS plc; (tr) Minale Tattersfield and Partners International Design Group; (bl) Neville Brody Graphic Design, London; (br) Saatchi & Saatchi International.

"Her hair that lay along her back
Was yellow like ripe corn."

Dante Gabriel Rosetti